# THE
# VILLAGE
# DOCTOR

# THE
# VILLAGE
# DOCTOR

## FRED ARCHER

ALAN SUTTON PUBLISHING LIMITED

First published in the United Kingdom in 1986
Alan Sutton Publishing Ltd · Phoenix Mill · Far Thrupp · Stroud
Gloucestershire

Reprinted 1995

British Library Cataloguing in Publication Data

Archer, Fred, *1915–*
The village doctor.
1. Ashton under Hill (Hereford and
Worcester) – Social life and customs
I. Title
942.4'49    DA690.A815

ISBN 0-86299-254-0

Typesetting and origination by
Alan Sutton Publishing Limited.
Photoset Imprint 12/13.
Printed in Great Britain by
WBC Limited, Bridgend.

# CONTENTS

# THE
# VILLAGE
# DOCTOR

# EDWARD ROBERSON, M.R.C.S.

Edward Roberson was the village doctor at Ashton-under-Hill for about forty years until his death in 1928. I knew him well when I was a boy. There was something very special about this old gentleman which smacked of an earlier age.

In the village he was revered, and respected by many of the men of the farms; a benevolent man who never sent his bill to the poor but counted on their votes when he stood for the District Council election. Doctor Roberson's patients were scattered around the Bredon Hill villages while some lived on the hill itself. The patients on the hill were visited by the doctor on horseback, more often than not in the dead of night. His theory was, 'See your patients at night, see them at their worst.'

A vivid picture of his son, Edward Buckram Roberson, flaxen haired and Norfolk jacketed, driving the doctor to the station in a high trap brings back a thrill difficult to explain. The horse, Lavender, stood between the shafts outside Rockland house waiting for the Master to climb on to the trap seat beside Buckram. The doctor was always late, for by then the train to Ashchurch would be steaming out of Hinton station two miles away. Buckram cracked his whip and the doctor held tight to the high trap seat as Lavender tried, as he had tried so many times, to race the train to Ashton station.

The village street was a dusty limestone track in summer, the stone from Bredon Hill pressed down by the constant stream of waggons going to and from the farms. Although the wheel ruts had been filled in by the roadmen, the track was uneven. Clay from the cartwheels mixed with the cow muck from two herds of milkers that passed twice a day to the milking sheds, and in winter the spring water running off the hill in little streams turned the mixture into a slush. This was the doctor's road to the station.

Buckram was young and lithesome and stood on the board in front of the trap like a Roman charioteer, fearless, steady as a rock as the trap swayed and bounced over the rough road. The doctor, by now an old man, held on, his sleepy face showing evidence of his habit of lying in bed till noon. As the father and son passed our house, Buckram gave Lavender an extra urge as the whip cracked – 'Think I stole you, you lazy beast!' The trap now rocked on its springs like a boat on a choppy sea. The train had reached Stanborrow Crossing and was slowing down towards the station. Lavender was fast losing the race; as the iron tyres of the trap went noisily across the gravelled station yard the little train puffed leisurely out of the station.

Doctor Roberson was allowed to board the Midland Railway train to Cheltenham in the siding, where a fairly long line of goods trucks stood, loaded with apples, Brussels sprouts and potatoes bound for markets in the north of England. At three o'clock every week-day afternoon a little tank engine hauled these trucks to Evesham where they were marshalled.

The engine driver's orders from 'The Company', on seeing Dr Roberson's trap charging full speed down Station Road, were to wait on the branch line where there was a gap between the trucks in the siding. Sometimes the siding was filled with other trucks, loaded with cattle cake from Gloucester, coal from the Forest of Dean, fertilizer from Avonmouth. On such days the doctor boarded the train further down the line near the allotments, which were dotted alongside the permanent way, half acre plots, one acre plots and some smaller pieces of land. When the railway company acquired the land in 1864 they often had to buy whole fields or pieces of fields. The land alongside the siding was about two acres long and narrow. A hut stood there where the platelayers had their lunch and kept their tools safely locked away: hedgehooks, crow-bars, spades, pickaxes and sledge-hammers, all used for maintaining the track. Bill Drinkwater's little coal wharf and hut were handy to where his truck of coal stood.

No one but the Doctor ever caught the train in the siding, not even the late squire who owned the adjoin-ing land or the vicar who journeyed regularly from Beckford to Ashton. Moncrief, Buckram's younger brother, told me how this came about. Doctor Roberson had been one of the chief surgeons employed by the old London & North Eastern Railway Company. In the early days of steam railway accidents were common – ghastly accidents with many folk injured. It was a time of trial and error; the signalling system was still in an experimental stage (the Great Western Railway were first in the field in perfecting a nearly foolproof signalling system). The early passen-ger coaches were made of wood, and when there was a train crash the wood splintered, the casualties were numerous. Doctor Roberson saved many lives at many train crashes, and witnessed some awful scenes when he was a surgeon in charge of first aid to the injured. Moncrief told me tales of how his father applied tourniquets to stem the flow of blood from severed limbs. Although the doctor worked for the London & North Eastern Railway his devotions and skill were common knowledge to the Midland Railway Company. In fact he worked among the injured at the scene of a railway accident near Bristol.

Dr Roberson's way of dress was as much a mark of his profession as the corduroys of the men of the fields. The doctor, when on his rounds, wore a black frock coat with cloth-covered buttons, and striped trousers which clung to his legs like six-inch drain-pipes at the bottom, but nicely shaped around the breech. His boots were black, buttoned at the side. The box hat, fashionable at the time, was not as deep as a topper. When out with the gun and Sailor, his spaniel dog, Doctor Edward looked like the farmers of the village, dressed in tweeds and a soft hat.

I watched the doctor working in his surgery under a window which was close to the roadside footpath. He appeared mystical to me as he mixed his medicines over a sink with a bucket of water beside him. His closely clipped King Edward VII beard under a grey moustache stained with nicotine fascinated me and fired my imagination; the smoking-cap, that he wore on his head smacked of the East. Was he a miracle man? Did his medicines grow from the herbs of the hill? He counted aloud as he mixed one spot of coloured liquid out of one bottle with a number of spots of some other potion. I could hear him counting from the footpath. The now shaking hand of a man of eighty allowed one spot too many to fall into the enamel bowl. 'Damn and blast,' he called out as he threw the whole mixture down the sink and started again to spot the potions into the measured spring water in the bowl.

This time his measurements were satisfying to him so he poured the mixture into a funnel which he fixed into the neck of the medicine bottle, filled the bottle and stuck on a label with instructions on it. He then covered the bottle with white paper, melted some sealing-wax to seal the edges, and someone's prescription was ready for collection. At six o'clock the villagers collected their cough mixtures, their jalap, and indigestion mixtures reeking of peppermint. 'Tell your father to give the bottle a thundering good shaking before he takes his medicine, boy,' I remember him saying.

Dr Roberson was an excellent shot. For many years he was a member of the London Rifle Brigade and won a silver cup for shooting. He loved his gun and his spaniel dog, and rented Mr Percy Attwood's shoot on the sixty acres adjoining Ashton Wood on the slopes of Bredon Hill where I farmed for thirty years.

What other doctor took his gun to visit his patients on his rounds, I wonder. My cousin George, who at that time lived at the Barracks, Kersoe, adjoining Percy Attwood's land, was ill with flu. The doctor arrived and, not waiting for an answer to his knock, walked straight in. George, who was sitting by his fireside, was confronted by the doctor carrying his gun. He looked up from his chair and, still feeling pretty low, said, 'You haven't come to shoot me Doctor?'

The old doctor's deafness caused many a laugh. 'How are you boy, I brought you into the world over twenty years ago.'

George replied, 'Oh, I'm better, but have a nasty boil on my neck.'

'Let your trousers down,' the doctor said, propping his gun in the corner of George's cottage sitting-room.

'My neck Doctor, MY NECK!' shouted George.

'Ah, a bread poultice with a little salt, as hot as you can bear it and I'll give you a tonic. You are run down my lad.' The doctor then walked home under the wood, not empty handed for his gun kept the family in rabbits and game throughout the season.

Doctor Roberson first came to live in the village in 1890, renting The Close, a rather grand black and white half-timbered farmhouse from Mr Attwood. He lived there alone apart from his dogs, kept his horse in the orchard and soon had a number of patients on his books from all around Bredon Hill. He drove his horse and high trap when visiting patients who lived on the flat land of the Vale, whilst the folk who lived on the hill were treated by this smart, good looking man coming on horseback. As the nearest doctor lived six miles away, Roberson's arrival at The Close was welcomed, especially by the old and the poor of the parish.

He soon got involved in village life as Treasurer at St Barbara's church. He then became Church Warden, and was the village representative on the Board of Guardians, the District Council, Parish Council, etc. This gave him a status in village life he never lost. He was opposed at an election for the District Council by an up-and-coming farmer. Edward Roberson won with a handsome majority. It's true the old and poor amongst his patients were reminded to vote for him when he did his rounds and were told that he had never sent them a bill, and neither would he if they voted for him at the election.

At that time the doctor was courting Amy, one of the five daughters of the late Thomas Baldwyn of Rockland House. His only son died whilst a pupil at Camden Grammar School, and Mrs Baldwyn had been left to cope with five daughters and a small farm. Amy was much younger than her suitor and her family tried to prevent the marriage.

# REVD WILLIAM HENRY MONCRIEF ROBERSON

The most interesting facets of the Roberson family were the eccentricities which permeated right the way through the nineteenth century and the early twentieth century. Edward's father, Revd William Henry Moncrief Roberson, was a conformist in the way he practised his religion yet radical in his life in the village and the diocese. He conformed because as a Clerk in Holy Orders he performed the duties he was supposed to, but his attitude was, do the minimum, a system of going through the motions. Revd Roberson seemed averse to singing in his church but at one stage in his ministry delighted in long sermons, sermons not so much gospel as asserting his loyalty to the Queen rather than God. Outspoken stuff. Jingoism.

William Henry Moncrief did have a great interest in the glebe land. He was probably a better farmer than rector. The whole crux of the Roberson philosophy can be summed up in these few words: they refused to be driven; driven into anything which they had not planned themselves. Lead them you could. I believe that they were basically generous folk, right the way through from William Henry Moncrief to Doctor Edward and latterly to William Moncrief.

Revd Roberson came to the living at Titherington in 1830, at the age of twenty-eight, and entered into a temporary agreement with the squire who was patron of the living. Squire Hardwick founded the Titherington quarries, and it was stone from there that was used in the construction of Avonmouth docks. He also started Titherington prize band (the brass band was the squire's pride and joy), and sponsored the local football teams, senior and junior. He had a sense of humour and named his teams The Pebbles, after the mineral wealth of the village.

Bill Cartes was one of Hardwick's employees in the quarry. He boasted that once he played cricket with the squire and E.M. Grace, a brother to the famous Dr W.G. Grace. The squire ruled Titherington as a good employer, yet tight in many ways – in ways of money and in his dictatorial manner as overseer of the church.

George Boyt, pork butcher and founder of the Baptist church, didn't get on with Squire Hardwick. George was a fine preacher and orator and a wit. His sermons were very much sermons which could be understood by the uneducated villagers of the time. Once he said that some men were like pigs – they never bothered to look up until they were on their backs. He resented the power and prestige of the rector and, in common with most non-conformists, he detested the system of the squire, the patron of the living, appointing a university man to the rectory. George could see that these men used the pulpit as a platform to tell the labourers that the existing order was God's will – the rich man in his place, the poor man at the gate.

Squire Hardwick had two nephews at Oxford university. The elder of the brothers was studying Holy Orders. When the squire made the agreement with William Henry Moncrief Roberson it was, as previously stated, a temporary agreement. This was to last until Squire Hardwick's elder nephew had finished his studies at university and could become Rector at Titherington. Hardwick was obviously planning to keep the living in the Hardwick family. Unfortunately the squire's elder nephew died before he had taken Holy Orders. The squire told Revd Roberson that he intended to substitute the younger nephew as Rector of Titherington. 'No,' Roberson said, 'I made the agreement to vacate the living when your elder nephew had taken Holy Orders. I shall not vacate the living in favour of anyone else.' The squire was furious. His wife wrote a pleading letter to Revd Roberson imploring him to let their younger nephew take the living. William Henry Moncrief Roberson was far from being humble. He, at twenty-eight years of age, considered himself to be on a par with the squire.

William Roberson was a scholar, a stickler for the letter of the law. His father had been Town Clerk of Oxford and in the capacity of a lawyer he had won a very important law suit for a friend. The beautiful inlaid mahogany dining suite which his friend gave him as a present for acting for him has been handed down through four generations.

Squire Hardwick found Roberson a man difficult to deal with – a man who would have the pound of flesh he was entitled to. Maybe if the squire had been more diplomatic, Roberson would have moved from the rectory. I wonder why Hardwick didn't offer young Roberson a sum of money to get out. What Hardwick did, however, was to aggravate Roberson. He knocked down the dividing wall between the rectory and the manor and had it rebuilt nearer to the rectory, thereby gaining more land for the manor gardens. Roberson did not object. The squire was possibly within his rights, for he owned the manor and was patron of the living – he had a claim on the rectory and the garden. He also filled in a duckpond on the rectory glebe land and made a garden there. Robersons have always been fond of ducks and no doubt Revd Roberson would have missed the pond. In later years his doctor son kept a lot of ducks; they used to swim in the roadside stream opposite Rockland House at Ashton-under-Hill. Edward had a similar setback when, despite his appeal, the stream was piped by the council. It used to run where the little bridges crossed it by the cottage gardens.

Revd Roberson dug his heels in and refused to budge. He declared that the only person entitled to make him vacate the living was the nephew who died. He was the man named in the document, signed by the squire and the rector. The tension grew, but all the time Revd Roberson kept his temper. That cool, calculating mind of his played a waiting game.

The manor and the rectory being adjacent properties tended to make the situation even more explosive. There was a short cut from the manor buildings through a door into the rectory land and the squire's cowman took the cows through that door twice a day for the morning and evening milking. This was a gentleman's agreement, but Squire Hardwick was no gentleman in Roberson's book. Revd Roberson locked the door. Squire Hardwick lost his temper and, taking an axe, smashed down the door. The cowman drove the cows through the doorway and, with the squire's approval, made them trample all over the rectory land and gardens.

This was the last straw as far as Roberson was concerned. He had bided his time, carrying the proverbial stone in his pocket and at last he was going to throw it. Revd Roberson took Council's Opinion and decided to sue Squire Hardwick for damages and trespass on his property. Squire Hardwick made a counter-claim, but Roberson won the day. The County Court awarded him damages and granted an injunction against Squire Hardwick, who was also made to restore the duckpond. To say that the squire was disgusted would be an understatement. He walked about Titherington like a man possessed. Never before had he been forced to bow down to the rector. He called the rector a young upstart and not fit to be the priest of Titherington.

The squire then sold the living. Who to, one can't hazard a guess, but he didn't want to be associated with Roberson or the church any longer, never attending again. Revd Roberson, for his part, didn't feel benevolent towards the village under such a squire. He did only the minimum at the church. While other villages were building church schools, Titherington was left without one because of Roberson's attitude – a 'don't care' attitude. A National School was built in 1878 and had no connection with the church.

Joseph Leech's newspaper articles, *Rural Rides*, were first published in the 1840s. Leech was a tall, red-headed Irishman who started a newspaper in Bristol. He wrote his articles under the guise of an old man, although he was then just thirty years of age. Calling himself a churchgoer he visited churches in the Bristol area and made very caustic comments on the parson, the clerk and the congregation. This comedy went on for a long time. Obviously the church folk were looking out for the man, but as Joseph described himself as being sixty years of age, portly, and wearing pince-nez glasses, they were unable to detect him.

Leech visited the church at Titherington on 10 October 1846. He had intended to go to Tortworth on his horse, John Bunyan, but found himself at Titherington. The village folk, when asked the time of the morning service, were loath to talk about the church or Revd Roberson. Some said they hadn't been to church since Roberson came. At the church Joseph Leech was surprised to find another parson in the pulpit. Revd Roberson had gone to Berkeley to do duty for Revd Seaton Karr and he had expected Revd Hicks from a neighbouring parish to do his duty. A search had been made for Revd Hicks, but without success, so a Mr Barker took the service.

The service was a charade without singing or a sermon; the clerk was uncouth and slovenly in his responses. Afterwards, a farmer in a blue coat told Joseph that had Revd Roberson taken the service he would have been quicker. 'Quicker,' Joseph said, 'Why, there was no singing, no sermon. Why doesn't Roberson have hymn singing?'

'Mr Honeywell offered to get some hymn-books,' the farmer said, 'but Revd Roberson does not see the use of hymns.'

Perhaps Roberson did preach at churches away from home. He left behind a stack of sermons he was supposed to have delivered. I wonder where Seaton Karr was on 10 October 1846. He was the illegitimate unacknowledged son of Lord Fitzharding of Berkeley

Castle – that's how he got the living at Berkeley. Soon after he ran off with a woman and left the town.

# EDWARD'S ENGAGEMENT TO IDA BARNARD

Edward Roberson was twenty-four when he received the first letter from Ida Barnard of White Notley, Witham, Essex. She was obviously very fond of Edward, and was concerned about his health and that he would not make himself ill again by overstudying.

White Notley
24 November 1870

My Dearest Edward,
I have a letter from Annie telling me that she will forward any letters that are sent to her.

Have you passed your examinations yet? Do not study so hard that you make yourself ill again.

I do not think anyone really suspects there is anything between us although Mamma occasionally tries to tease me about you. I say tease, because of course it does not tease me, it rather pleases me.

I shall only be able to send one envelope this time for I find the one I have directed will not hold more. It is alright its not being black edged because I have given up writing to Annie on black edged paper.

With my *best* love,
Believe me
Dearest Edward
Ever your loving Ida.

It would appear from the letter that she had already known Edward for some time. He had not yet obtained a practice and was living at the rectory at Titherington. He had stayed at White Notley with the Barnard family. Ida was a wealthy young lady, eleven years his junior, and although she and Edward were engaged her frequent illness postponed their marriage. Their letters to each other were few and far between, and one feels that Edward had other lady friends in Gloucestershire.

In 1881 Edward was about to leave Titherington and take a practice at Frome in Somerset. Ida was worried because Edward threatened to go to America. There had apparently been a wet harvest, and this, following the disastrous summer of 1879, worried Ida. She had become ill and her handwriting was shaky.

31 August 1881

My Dearest Edward,
I hope although I have not been able to write sooner you will have my letter alright.

Perhaps when you leave Titherington, which I know you will be sorry to do, you will feel less despondent. When you hint of leaving England it seems that everyone has the same idea for many have gone lately, though none in your capacity. Things have not been very promising of late, so many homes are broken up. When one constantly hears of these things it does not tend to raise the spirits.

How will you manage about harvesting your barley if this wet weather continues? I am afraid you will find it troublesome and William [Partridge] will be alone in his shooting. I imagine you will soon be going into Somerset [Frome]. It strikes me that I shall not be able to write many more letters. However I shall not give it up until I am obliged to, for I like having letters too well.

With love from your loving Ida.

The harvest at Titherington was now Edward's responsibility. His father had given up the living that year, after fifty-one years as rector, but the Robersons still lived in the rectory. Ida need not have been concerned that the wet harvest would prevent Edward from shooting. He would make time to be out with his gun regardless of sodden sheaves in the stooks at Titherington glebe. Edward and his gun were a major part of life in the parish until he died. The shoots at Ashton of the hand-reared pheasants driven over the guns would never have had such good bags without Edward – the men who came from Birmingham with their fancy Purdy twelve bores managed to bring a few birds down, but it was Edward who was the crack shot. Many a time he smiled to himself as he stood with the young bloods from that Midland city dressed up in their breeches and Norfolk jackets like a dog's dinner. 'Huh', he said to his farmer friend, Sam, 'they couldn't hit a barn if they were inside it.'

Ida's handwriting had improved, when, on 26 December 1887, she wrote to Edward concerning his health:

My Dear Edward,
Now really, take my advice and wear a nutmeg, you will get quite well. I did when I wore one. [Nutmeg was an old remedy for rheumatism.]

It does seem that Edward's love-life ebbed and flowed between several ladies. On 4 December 1879 Edward had a decidedly stinging letter from Amy Rowlatt. Edward had more or less promised marriage to her despite the fact that he was in constant touch by letter and by his frequent visits with Ida Barnard. Ida was much better off financially than Amy Rowlatt, but she was an invalid for years.

4 December 1879

My Dear Mr Roberson,

I really do not know how to answer your letter. You have not offended me, but I still continue to think that you have not stuck to the truth exactly.

I acknowledge that I did show my feelings *perhaps too much* during the latter part of your stay in Hatfield and also when you came to see me, but I did not know that it *mattered*. I cared for you very much and I thought you did for me.

I understood that if you could honourably break off the engagement with Miss Barnard (I think her name is) that you would have asked me to be your wife. It seems that I was wrong. As for Papa, he is not so anxious to get rid of me as you insinuate. I do not remember his coupling our names together but once.

You ask me why I did not write before. Because I kept hoping that you would either come or write and when two years had nearly gone and I had heard nothing from you I came to the conclusion that you had quite ceased to care for me and thought that the most sensible thing I could do would be to try and forget you. It was no means an easy task and I think would have taken me a long time but for your own *unkind* letters.

You say I call you no gentleman and a speaker of untruths. Excuse me, I did nothing of the kind. I simply said what I still think, that some parts of your letter were neither true nor gentlemanly. Perhaps you will say that is a distinction without a difference. I do not think so and if you recollect all you put in your first letter to me I think in your own heart you will acknowledge me to be in the right. You are quite wrong in what you say about my reasons for writing to you. I wrote to learn your true feelings toward me, you have completely misjudged me. I should never marry merely for money. I have often told you that unless I loved anyone very dearly I would not have him for my husband. What you say about my wishes with regard to yourself and being betrothed is horrible. I assure you I cherish no unkind thoughts with regards to Miss Barnard, nor ever have. You say you were sorry that she was ill, and of course I concluded that wished her to get well so that you could be married. I think you told me that she had money and as you say you shall never marry anyone who has none, I suppose she is just what you want. With reference to myself, I shall always continue your friend. I wish you well in every *possible* way. Your letter from beginning to end is unkindness itself but the end hurt me more than anything. It shows *what* you take me for and as such is the case I think it is a good thing that we are parted and never likely to see each other again.

I have loved you Edward with all my heart and gone through *not* a *little* unhappiness for your sake. As I said before, I shall always be your sincere friend, but never, even if you wished it, would be your wife. I have no thoughts of being married to anyone else at present. My address will be c/o J.W. Page, Swalcliffe, Nr. Banbury Oxon.

Always yours most sincerely,
Amy M. Rowlatt.

Very little other correspondence survives for the next few years. Ida continues to live as a severe invalid and presumably Edward has dabbled elsewhere apart from the illuminating case of Amy Rowland. A letter from Isaec Pleomock, a neighbour, shows that Edward was taking some of the responsibility for his father's glebe land. His letter, written Gloucester fashion, is dated 1 July 1884.

## THE VILLAGE DOCTOR

Titherington

Dear Sir,
I have just thought of your clover and we have the first cut and will be able to finish it all next week if the weather do hold good, and I think you will be the luckiest man in the parish if you shall have another fine week therefore you can send to me before Saturday and tell me how many acors it is. We have beine verry buisy at my clover and have got it up this day and have three grownds of English about now. Your rye is got very long and I think that you will have a fair crop and trust you will make it well. Trusting you are well and shall be glad to hear from you.

I am Dr Sir, your truly,
Isaec Pleomock.

P.S. The young Esq is no better but is brother is glad to have a night at Titherington by hisself. Mr Jackson has almost got over his honeymoon and I think the Esq is the same.

On 9 December 1888 Ida wrote her last letter, being very ill.

My Dear Edward,
I do wish I could walk and see like other people. At times like the present I feel that I should be suffocated with the desire to be of some use. Mamma has gone away for a few days and here am I stationary except when I choose to take an airing in the donkey cart; quite an event.

Have you seen the Lancet lately? There is an advertisement about the Braintree Union.

With fondest love
Your loving Ida.

Ida Barnard died soon after, thus ending eighteen years of courtship. By her description of her illness it appeared that she had multiple sclerosis.

After living in Frome for a few years, Edward considered taking up a practice at Corse Lawn, near Gloucester. It was the doctor's wife who corresponded with Edward regarding the purchase of the practice:

Corse Grange
7 October 1884

The practice is in a pleasant country district within a short distance of Gloucester. An old established unopposed practice, the average cash receipts of which for the past three years amount to five hundred pounds per annum inclusive of appointments worth two hundred and thirty-one pounds. The district contains a population of five to six thousand and there is no opposition within five miles. Nearest railway station, five miles. Class of patients consist of clergy, farmers, etc. and the lowest visiting fee is five shillings, midwifery ten-and-six to two guineas, from twenty to thirty cases yearly.

One horse can work the practice.

There is a good family residence held at forty-five pounds per annum. Premium five hundred pounds, two hundred and fifty down and balance on the terminal of an introduction to meet the wishes of purchaser. Good hunting and shooting to be had.

Truly yours,
E. Broughton.

Letters went to and fro between Edward and Mrs Broughton. The final letter, dated 8 December 1885 reads:

Doctor Roberson's brothers,
Clement and Captain Thomas
Roberson, and right, his sister,
Phylis Margaret in 1886

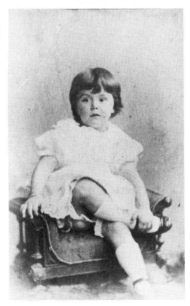

*Above*: members of the Baldwyn family at The Croft, Ashton

*Left*: Amy Baldwyn

Corse Grange
Nr. Gloucester

Dear Sir,
In answer to your letter this morning, I am to tell you
that my husband will not entertain the idea of three
hundred and fifty pounds unless we are paid a generous deposit to meet my husband as regard to terms, I
think we shall have to remain here where we are.

I am very sorry that you have been put to so much
trouble in answering my letters, for it all amounts to
nothing. I can only hope that for you it may turn out to
be all for the best. You will be able to continue your
studies and I trust may meet with a pratice to suit you.

One thing is quite certain, that in this world we are
not to have it all our own way.

Believe me,
Dear Sir,
Yours Truly,
E. Broughton

In 1886 Edward was appointed Assistant Medical
Officer of Health for Hatfield in Hertfordshire, a very
important post. He was also employed by the old
London and North Eastern Railway Company as a surgeon and attended the injured at many bad railway accidents. A member of the London Rifle Brigade for many
years, he became a splendid shot, and won a silver cup.

# EDWARD'S ENGAGEMENT AND MARRIAGE TO AMY BALDWYN

Edward Roberson came to live at The Close,
Ashton-under-Hill, in 1890 and started a medical
practice in a village where no doctor had practised

before. By the winter of 1891 Edward was secretly courting Amy Baldwyn. In January 1892 Amy wrote to Edward four times.

> Dovedale,
> Blockley.
> 1 January 1892

Dear Dr Roberson,

I am again at Blockley as you will see by my letter. I came yesterday. I could not leave before as the weather was so wretched the day before. Mother seemingly had a private interview with you which I know very little about. One thing I know, she told you that I was going to Beckford which I did consent to go later on if I did return. [To her sister Mrs Nind's house.]

I feel that I get into worse trouble every day and I almost wish that 'peaceful death' would come and end my existence. I cannot think what good I was sent into this world for.

Wishing you the compliments of the season,

> Yours sincerely,
> Amy Baldwyn

One may wonder why poor Amy sent the compliments of the season on January 1st. The Baldwyn family celebrated Christmas on Old Christmas Day, January 6th.

> Dovedale,
> Blockley.
> 8 January 1892

Dear Dr Roberson,

I am pleased by your letter you will be willing for my visit to Quinton. I have decided to go on Monday as a dinner party is to take place during the week. Perhaps my services may be some help.

I will assure you I will not allow my cousin to interfere with me about getting me a suitor there will not be, as I was never introduced to anyone there that I should care to associate with longer than the evening.

I expect when you hear from me again I will be at Quinton.

Yours very sincerely,
Amy Baldwyn


Quinton House
Stratford-on-Avon
17 January 1892

Dear Dr Roberson,
As I am not going to church this evening owing to a slight cold I thought I would spend the time in writing to you. What dreadful sad news we have heard about our young Prince and what a trial it will be for the Royal Family and especially Princess May. It seems to have cast a gloom everywhere, but I suppose Royalty have trials to bear as well as us other people. The country at large seems to be in a distressing state. [This refers to the Prince of Wales' elder son Albert Victor who died 14 January 1892.] I do not like the sound of one *little word* in your last letter. You may guess what it is Sir. You must learn to express yourself milder, but then you will say I am dictating to you again.

We have been busy this last day or two contriving for the dinner party which took place Thursday. Tomorrow I am going to Blockley in order to fetch my painting as I have left most of my luggage there.

There is a gentleman (Mr Baker) in the room while I am writing this letter. He is asking me if I am writing about smashed turnips. I do not exactly know what he means. Rop [a cousin] is writing to Mother, I have seen that it's alright.

Yours very sincerely,
Amy Baldwyn

Quinton House
23 January 1892

Dear Dr Roberson,

I am as naughty as usual and not gone to church again this evening but it is cousin Rop's fault as she wanted me to keep her company. I have been writing to some friends so I thought that I would write to you.

If I see your Mother and Sister at Bristol I shall be quite satisfied without visiting your other Sister at Clifton. As I wrote in my last letter I think that it would be wise to go to Bristol and back again to Quinton on the same day. If you would permit me I could go down to Bristol alone and introduce myself to them. If you would write to them first then we could arrange other affairs afterwards. I suppose it would not matter *where* the eventful ceremony took place, and then go to Clifton again. [What a disappointment for Amy not to be married at St Barbara's church, Ashton-under-Hill, where the Baldwyn family had worshipped for five hundred years.]

You seem to be working hard. They cannot get doctors around here for love or money, so many cases.

I have put my frizzley wig up today under the tuition of Rop. I do miss it so as I am afraid I shall get influenza at the back of my neck. I have been so teased and insulted about it so I thought I would put it up finally.

Yours very sincerely,
Amy Baldwyn

The letter of 17 January contains a hint 'I do not like the sound of one *little word* . . .' of the volcanic troubles to come. However, Amy wrote to Edward's mother on 6 February 1892 to ask for an interview:

c/o T.C. Hiatt, Esq.,
Quinton House,
Nr. Stratford-on-Avon
6 February 1892

Dear Mrs Roberson,
I have not the pleasure of knowing you so therefore I must apologise for the great liberty I am taking upon myself in writing to you. I assure you it is of very great importance. Your son Edward Roberson has offered his intentions to me, I believe he has told you.

All my relations are objecting greatly to our engagement and will not hear of it, chiefly I think, because they know nothing of his family and also the difference between our age. Therefore, it is my one wish and desire to see you if you will permit me before any decision takes place. I have no father nor brother living to help me in this affair, so I think the wisest plan I can do is to have a little talk with you.

Your son has told me you are in delicate health and I know new faces and company will be trying for you, so I will make my visit as short as possible and only visit you for the day and then only for a short time.

As my journey will be rather long, so as not to inconvenience you in the slightest, I shall return to my cousins the same day.

Any day will suit me that is convenient to you.

Yours very sincerely,
Amy Baldwyn

The reply to Amy's letter must have been favourable as shortly afterwards she went to Bristol to meet Mrs

Roberson. On 4 March 1892 everything looked very unsettled. The family difficulties on Amy's part seemed certain to put an end to the engagement.

Quinton House,
4 March 1892

Dear Dr Roberson,
Rop wishes not to have anything to do with me or you in the affair and that is why she has not fixed a day for you to spend at Quinton, so I am leaving here on Monday as it is best not to stay anywhere you are not welcome yourself.

I am going to stay at Beckford for only a short time. You may be sure they are all anxious to get me into a situation as soon as possible. I decidedly should so that I may be out of the way of my relations. You said you would be decidedly angry if I did. Well I cannot help myself as yet and shall get in to something next week if possible.

I suppose I must say goodbye as I know this stupid net of mine will cut our friendship and I know I cannot hear from you at Beckford, and I shall not go to Ashton, as I promised you that I should never return there unless things were different.

Yours very sincerely,
Amy Baldwyn

Amy did return to Ashton-under-Hill sometime later and Edward, who was living at Hampton, near Evesham, married her at Hampton parish church by Licence. He spent the previous night to the wedding in Ashton-under-Hill at Mr Attwood's farmhouse known as The Close, then walked on the morning of the wedding the five miles along the railway line from Ashton to Hampton. Amy bought a train ticket to

Evesham, so that the family would believe she was off shopping, but got off the train at Hampton.

---

By Licence

Hampton Parish Church

Edward Roberson aged forty-nine years
Bachelor surgeon
Residence at the time of marriage: Hampton
Father's name: William Henry Moncrief
   Roberson
Profession: Clerk in Holy Orders
Amy Baldwyn Spinster, twenty-one
Residence: Ashton-under-Hill
Father: Thomas Baldwyn, Gentleman
Married in Parish Church according to the
Rites and Ceremonies of the Church of England.


By me, J.G. Knapp,
in the presence of Martin Wilson and E.
Merryweather

---

After the wedding Edward and Amy went on honeymoon to Edward's mother's house at Clifton, Bristol, and on their return they lived for a while at The Close as tenants of Mr Attwood. The Baldwyn family were furious and only Bunch, Amy's younger sister, stood by the newly-wed pair. They were never to forgive Amy for marrying a man nearing fifty – almost twice her age.

It is not clear when Amy and Edward moved to Rockland House, the home of Mrs Baldwyn. Rockland

House held many unpleasant memories for Amy – she had been badly treated by her mother, and by her cousins, who lived in the Cotswolds. If she had had the support of her mother and cousins, Amy may have been better equipped to deal with a hot-tempered, womanising husband. One may be sure that Edward had been around a bit; he had played the field. When I knew him he was an old man, with a distinguished air about him and a face of great character.

It is doubtful if Amy had ever had a suitor before Edward came along. She would not have had much opportunity with the Baldwyn clan keeping her on the straight and narrow. Edward, who had had twenty-two years courting all and sundry, came to the village like a lightning flash. He was soon involved in the church, the school and the Parish Council, as usually happened when a man of education came to live in a village community. In coming to Ashton-under-Hill and marrying Amy, Edward, a foreigner from Titherington with no real roots in the land, found himself up against the whole Baldwyn empire.

It would be unfair to say that Edward was marrying Amy Baldwyn for her money, but this did have a bearing on it. The Baldwyn family had been very rich indeed. They were both landowners and property owners. They had estates apart from Ashton-under-Hill. Thomas Baldwyn, Amy's father, died quite young leaving five daughters. The only son died while at school. Thomas's widow had been robbed by an unscrupulous solicitor from Evesham. To be fair to Edward, he did try and sort out this fraud for his mother-in-law.

The lords of the manor were Baldwyns, and were close relatives of Amy. William Henry, the squire, had been fabulously rich, but had squandered his fortune in the markets and fairs as his mental state became progressively worse. By 1892 he had been put in the charge of two 'keepers'. It is said that his mental condition was the result of intermarriage between cousins. He was getting quite dangerous with his gun. His pursuits of imaginary birds and beasts on Bredon Hill at night with Uncle Jim and some of the young fellows from the villages are legendary. When Uncle asked Squire William Henry Baldwyn for a rise in wages he was refused. Uncle made his request because he and Austin Stevens were doing the heavy work of sack-carrying and earning the same wages as old men on two sticks. After a pause, the squire fetched his gun from the manor and, producing a handful of cartridges from his pocket, gave them to Uncle Jim. From another pocket the squire took out a little money-bag containing one hundred sovereigns. 'Here Jim, take my gun and these cartridges and there's one hundred sovereigns if you will go and shoot Doctor Roberson.'

Why this resentment to the doctor, this hostility? The squire was, as the local farm labourers said, 'Gone off his yud', yet there was another reason for this bad blood between Roberson and Baldwyn. He resented the match between Amy and Edward because he felt that this middle-aged doctor was marrying young Amy in order to have a stake in the Baldwyn fortune.

Edward Roberson was a man of the people, liked, even loved, by the labourers and their wives. He had tried to save some of the arthritic elderly men from having to work for the squire. They stood ankle deep in ditches, hedging and ditching and draining the squire's land. 'I have had the best out of you and now I'll have the worst,' the squire often said. Yet if Edward Roberson had had his way and rescued these old men from the labour of the land, one thing was sure – instead of working for ten shillings a week, these men would have been given parish relief of half a crown a week by the Guardian of the Poor, John Baldwyn. If they were not satisfied with this, there was always the workhouse, known in the village as Hampton Addleton or Hampton Headland, the headland being the boundary of a field where the plough horses turned.

Who paid for parish relief, you may well ask. The ratepayers, and the squire was the biggest ratepayer. Supposing the squire himself had attempted to shoot Doctor Roberson. I know who would have been quickest on the draw; Edward of course. No better man than he has ever shot the pheasant in the rides of Ashton wood.

John Baldwyn, of Holloway Farm, was a gentleman farmer and Guardian of the Poor. His eldest son was at the Manor Farm trying to rescue some of the live and dead stock belonging to the squire. John Baldwyn hunted with the parson, Revd Harrison, and together they could be seen at the races – a sporting pair. They overstepped the mark when they put heavy bets on a loser of the French Derby. It seemed that as Edward Roberson infiltrated into the scene at Ashton the Baldwyn fortune was waning.

In July 1894, two years after their wedding, Edward and Amy had a bitter disappointment. Amy wrote to old Mrs Roberson from Ashton:

30 July 1894

Dear Mrs Roberson,
My confinement took place about half past ten on last Saturday night. I had a nice big boy, Roberson-like in appearance with curlish light hair. Much to Edward's and my great disappointment he was born dead.

Edward thinks he had been dead for about a week. My confinement came on rapidly so that everything had ended before the other medical man could get there and Edward gave me all the help I needed. I have a good nurse with me and am very well under the circumstances.

They are going to put the little fellow in the churchyard this afternoon so I am feeling a little sad. With love to yourself and Mary,

Yours affectionately,
Amy Roberson

Amy was quite ill for a time and by December was away from Ashton staying with friends. Edward wrote:

Ashton,
5 December 1894

My Dear Amy,
I was very glad to hear you are improving in health. I had a card from my sister yesterday to say mother was very ill, would I come. I telegraphed to Mary to know the rights of it and had a letter this morning to say mother had had a very bad attack of vomiting and faintness which as she was then better deemed to be a bilious attack, so I shall not go now. I am very busy and should have written yesterday.

I was chairman of the Parish Meeting at the School Room last night for the election of Parish Councillors. In consequence I have had a good bit to do in writing formal letters and filling up forms today. Will write again. Meanwhile let me know how you are from day to day. Johnson [the servant] will go by the 5.26 train today. (The sock came in very handy.)

With my very best love dear Amy,

Yours, Edward

# AMY

I do remember Amy. As a small boy I saw her often sitting on a chair underneath the pear tree opposite Rockland House. She was by then an invalid, looked after by her daughters.

*31*

Amy's marriage to Edward was stormy at times, according to Edward's diary. I think Doctor Edward was intolerant, insensitive to Amy, who after all was half his age. It was as if he treated her little better than the servant girls in the house. It's pretty obvious that the servants were treated as sexual playthings at times. No wonder Amy would go for days without speaking to her husband.

After Amy had the stillborn boy in July 1894 she gave birth to a girl, Mary, on 7 June 1895. On 17 February 1896 Mr Milton, an artist, took a photograph of the baby girl. On that same day Edward wrote in his diary:

*17th Feb.* Violent passion accompanied with vehement askerveration[?] and gesticulation that she, Mrs Amy Roberson, would never make another pigeon pie because I called her attention to the fact that the breasts were all together on one side of the pie and the wings, legs and hardbacks on the other side whereas they should have been uniformly distributed.

The selected few diary entries following are obviously one-sided but illuminate the volcanic life led by Edward and Amy, the result of the mixed eccentricities of both families.

*16th March* Attended Parish Meeting. Confronted by illiterate rogues.

*17th March* Went to Clifton [his mother's sale]. Servant girl came to Rockland House. Jane Reim left and went to Mrs Tindale.

*19th March* Jane Reim went to Union House at Evesham accompanied by Nind and Bunchie Baldwyn [Amy's sister].
   'Here endeth her drinking and cheating Fox caught in its own trap.'

[Jane had lived at the doctor's house as housekeeper, and apparently robbed him.]

*19th March*   I swore at Ben my brother and told him to go to a warm climate (hell), and then bought the Corbell chairs off him.

*21st March*   Returned from Clifton at seven a.m. Saw Mother's face drop in thoughts as I left.

*22nd March*   Mrs Roberson violent and abusive because I bought the furniture thinking to please her.

*23rd March*   Mrs Roberson violent and abusive because I would not have a sofa carried upstairs in the dark because the stairs were steep and difficult and there was a difficult turning at the top. I then took the sofa into the dining room.

*Tuesday 24th March*   Mrs Roberson a little more placid.

*2nd April*   Mrs Roberson accused me of pinching the housekeeper at Rockland House, a favourite, and taking heed that for her text worked herself up into the customary volley of accusations, threats and abuse.

She is as impudent and vulgar as ever. She began it before breakfast upstairs. She arose savage and has gone to bed savage. She appears always savage. I have had such a doing of it. May fate bring me a remedy.

*3rd April*   Good Friday (God be praised).

*7th May*   Gave the girl Ellen Hale notice to leave.

*5th June*   Went to Clifton on 8.50 train. Saw mother and Ben. Took my child Mary, stayed the night with Amy. The poor child Mary weary and asleep at the station. Returned to Rockland House by the five o'clock train from Bristol but went to Clifton and saw Mother and Ben, but did not speak to the latter.

*23rd June*   Went to Clifton.

*24th June*   Had letter from Mrs Roberson!!!!!

*10th October*   Jeens my servant paid me one shilling and six pence for tooth drawing. [Doctor Roberson took teeth out for the villagers who could not get to an Evesham dentist.]

*30th December*   Mrs Roberson kicked me three times.

*8th July*   Mrs Roberson struck Mary the little child with her clenched fist with all her force in the middle of the back. The child being knelt forward and naked on the bed and was unaware of her attack because the child was playing with the baby powder box. She would not take any breakfast afterwards and was white, pale and feeble with movements for some hours afterwards.

*17th July*   Mrs Roberson violent and said she would not give thanks to the Almighty if I had never returned yesterday and she would never see me again. She is jealous of all the women imaginable. A jealous time, I have the need of the presence of women. It is nothing but women, women, women, and that I am wench-struck, all the while.

*30th August*   Mrs Roberson while I was chopping a bone up for the dog on the furnace at the back of the house in the dark, crept up and struck me a violent blow with her clenched fist in the angle of the jaw. No cause assigned beyond the customary hallucinations and jealousy of every servant we have. She calls the servant my mistress and myself a whore, continually refuses to eat and drink or leave the house. It's impossible to live with her. She has become terribly dangerous, savages the little weak child continually [Mary].

These one-sided accounts conflict with other accounts of Amy's character. It is a great shame that Amy did not keep a diary to reflect the other side of the coin.

Amy was essentially a good woman. She had strange, eccentric ways. This trait was, as in the case of the squire, due to inter-marriage in the Baldwyn family. Two of her sisters were mentally deranged, yet her other sisters, Bunch and Mrs Nind, were very capable ladies. This branch of the Baldwyn clan was artistic. Amy was no mean artist in water colours, and painted landscapes of Bredon Hill country. She was also very musical, and set the words of the old Ashton carols to music.

My cousins spoke in glowing terms of Amy. My father was the youngest of a family of eleven and married late, so all my cousins were much older than me. They served in the First World War, and had been patients of Doctor Roberson. When cousin Tom was in France he had regular parcels of food and cigarettes from Amy. She was so good to the soldiers. Bill Vale, now eighty-three, tells me that Amy was a great loyalist, and got the village women knitting socks and scarves for the troops. She organised this in Albany Vale's cottage.

St Barbara's church choir was never better served than when Amy was organist and conductor. The fact that the Baldwyns had lived in Ashton for five hundred years came through in Amy's life. This was the Baldwyns' village. They cared for the people and the church. It must have been hurtful for Amy when Edward was not accepted by the various branches of the Baldwyn family, both in her village and on the Cotswolds.

# DOCTOR ROBERSON'S PRACTICE

There is no doubt that Edward Roberson's life in the village was a very busy one. As Amy had no surviving brothers, it was Edward who took over Thomas Baldwyn's land and property within the parish. A great deal of his work as a doctor was done during the night, leaving the daylight hours for farming, council, and comittee work. However, his first love was his gun, and he always found time for shooting.

When the local landowner organised a shoot the guns were pretty pathetic, apart from one or two of the farmers. Edward was placed a little behind the line of shooters and in this position he bagged more pheasants than the rest of the syndicate. His left and right barrel rarely missed two birds.

One incident still remembered was when a deer strayed on the doctor's hill. The doctor's hill was a ten acre field alongside Gossle (Goose Hill), well clothed with bramble and gorse and alive with rabbits. General Davies, who owned the park at Elmley, had a herd of deer. Many years previously they had broken the fence and escaped. When the snow lay thick on the ground and the willows beside the stream were white with hoar frost the deer would venture towards the village stealing cabbage, pulling at hay-ricks and feeding on the doctor's hill.

Late one winter afternoon, as the dusk crept spookily over the gorse and bramble, a village chap saw what appeared to be a deer grazing alongside the Gossle hedge on the doctor's hill. The fellow ran down to the surgery and said, 'Doctor, thurs a deer on your hill.'

'Thank you lad; tell me where.'

'Alongside Gossle.'

The clipped, bearded, Victorian gentleman in breeches and gaiters and still wearing his smoking-cap, crept alongside Gossle hedge with his favourite double-barrelled Purdy shot-gun. He had number four shot in the cartridge in his bag, ammunition which, aimed at the heart, would kill a stag at thirty yards. Taking aim at the motionless object, he shot. The object stood defiant, so number two barrel was emptied of it's lead, but still the deer refused to fall. In the twilight Edward walked up to his prey, only to find it was not one of General Davies' escapees, but a wooden cow-crib which had been used to fodder a horse.

One wonders how the story got around, but it did. Maybe the lad who told the doctor of the deer followed him up the hill. A few days later a man collecting rags, bones and rabbit skins pulled up in the yard of the Plough and Harrow at lunchtime. 'Rags, bones, and rabbit skins!' – that cry had echoed all up the village street where women came out of their cottages and got a penny or two for a rabbit skin. At the Plough and Harrow not one of the customers had a rabbit skin to sell. One of Mr Hooper's regulars, a carter from Holloway Farm, said to the rag and bone man, 'I do know a gentleman who has a very fine deer skin he would like to sell. He lives at Rockland House.' Doctor Roberson came to the front door of his house and seeing this somewhat ragged man standing there, thought he was a patient, a casualty of the land. 'Well, what's wrong with you my lad?' the doctor said gruffly, still munching at his mid-day bread and cheese.

'Nothing sir, but I understand you have a deer skin to sell.'

The doctor flew into a rage and the man ran back towards the Plough and Harrow. 'Come back here,' the doctor shouted. 'Who told you of the deer skin, ay?'

'A chap at the pub said you had one.'

The doctor strolled across to his friend Mr Hooper and said, 'What's the game Bill, sending that man to see me?'

'Oh, it wasn't me who sent him Edward, just one of the village folk, and it wouldn't be fair to let on who it was. Some folk have a strange sense of humour.'

The doctor burst out laughing and suggested to Bill Hooper that he should treat him to a pint of his best Flowers beer.

Thomas Packer of Cheltenham was a great friend of Dr Roberson and it was he who started the Sick and Dividend Society. Dr Roberson was the official doctor who vetted the members for what was known as 'The Club'. It was bad luck if a member fell ill during the first months of the year, for there was little in the kitty to pay out benefit. Every Christmas the club members met at the Star Inn and shared what was left of the year's income.

The Club Feast, held on Trinity Monday, began with a service in St Barbara's church. The members then marched with their brass-mounted staves up the village street to Corse Lawn band. Every farmer, almost every householder, placed jugs of beer or cider on their garden walls for the members to refresh themselves. The feast was held in a marquee in the Plough and Harrow yard, and here Edward Roberson took the chair, accompanied by the vicar and John Baldwyn. Toasts were proposed and the doctor, in one parish magazine, remarked on the goodwill and sobriety of the members.

The National Health was in its infancy, and the club provided a safety net for the folk stricken with ill-health. When a few young men in their teens requested to join the club, Dr Roberson arranged a vetting in his consulting room. The figure of Edward in black cloth buttoned jacket and pin-striped trousers standing in this room with its thick, flowery wallpaper, old suite, and leather couch, commanded respect from the villagers. The youths stood in the hall, apprehensive of what would happen when the stethescope lay cold on the chest, and the old man made utterances which only he could understand. The curtains remained undrawn, and a knot of impish, inquisitive youths peered through the window as Edward vetted the potential club members. They stood naked in the candlelight as Edward, with another candle, searched their bodies, dropping hot wax in quite sensitive places.

'Rheumatic fever, where did you get that?' Edward asked a man in his twenties.

'In the army, Doctor,' the man replied.

'I'll pass you for the club; you are good for a few years yet.' Tom got his enrollment card.

Edward was also the medical man for the Beckford Sick and Dividend Club. Late one night a call came to Rockland House for the doctor to come urgently to the cottage where John Crump's cowman lived. Lavender was put in the shafts of the trap and Edward drove down Rabbit Lane to Malt House Row. It was just as well Lavender knew the way, for Edward had drunk more than was good for him on a dark January night. He tied Lavender up to some railings by the gate to Wilson Bedenham's farm. He entered the cottage and called upstairs. The cowman's wife answered, 'Come up Doctor.'

'Where's Bill, it's him I want to see', the doctor replied.

By then Bill's wife had got back into bed with her husband, who was steaming with sweat, a typical case of bronchial pneumonia. 'Out of bed Missus, I don't want you,' the doctor ordered. She went out on to the landing. The doctor knelt down beside Bill's bed. Bill felt better already, thinking the doctor churchwarden was about to say a prayer for his recovery. Holding himself tight around his middle the doctor's voice cried out, 'Where's the pot Bill, I do want to use it badly!' Bill signalled to the pretty pink flowered chamber standing on the ledge under the marble-topped washstand. The doctor grabbed the chamber-pot and relieved himself and only then did he examine Bill and from his pocket produced his famous mixture of drugs in a bottle.

It was impracticable for Edward to drive the horse and trap up the steep slopes of Bredon Hill, so he would visit the shepherds' cottages or gamekeeper's house on horseback, his Gladstone bag slung in front of the saddle. The outlying places all had picturesque names; Cobblers Quar, La Lu, Sheldon, Pidgeon Lane, Parsons Folly. Edward was a lifeline – not a flying doctor, yet always on call especially at night. He cared and kept many a man from a workhouse destiny.

Edward always enjoyed the ride as Lavender picked her way down the steep slopes from Cobblers Quar in the small hours of the morning, after Joe Whittle the gamekeeper had been attended to. Even more so, he enjoyed riding up the village street – he had said many times that he never went to bed until all the rogues and vagabonds were asleep. He stabled Lavender just across the road from Rockland House. Here, in a paddock where the perry pears grew and a cider mill stood alongside the stable, Sailor, his gun dog, kept guard.

Edward had never gone in for modern conveniences at Rockland House so the old two seater privy under the slate roof served the family. Crossing the road to the privy was public yet accepted. Accepted as much as fetching buckets of water from the roadside standpipe. Change came very slow to Rockland House until much later.

After the birth of Mary, Amy had two sons and three more daughters. The sons, Edward Buckram and

William Moncrief, grew up a couple of independent small yeoman farmers. The doctor, who found himself with a young family while almost at retirement age, had taken little notice of their education and offered them no help in following a career. Amy was often ill, which resulted in the boys having to leave school. There appeared to be money for the boys to pursue a very hit and miss agricultural life. Moncrief at one stage favoured the law, but never quite accomplished his aim to be a barrister.

Buckram, that blond-haired, mischievous son of the soil, was a law unto himself. He dabbled in dealing in the cattle markets, meeting farmers at the Railway Inn at Evesham and bringing the odd couple of calves home in his float. He soon set up as a dairyman, buying Devon cows to produce the milk for his round. His Cotswold-tiled cowshed was alongside the railway line, away from hard roads. Bob, his light brown cob, waited, while Buckram milked and filled the churns ready for his rounds. Bob waited, as Lavender waited for the doctor; father and son were always late. In competition with another dairyman, it was Buckram who gained the custom of the old folk of the village, for the cream on the Devon milk was rich. Delivery-time became guesswork. It could be anytime from seven in the evening till after midnight, so Buckram became known as the midnight milkman. He prided himself that it was his milk that fed the baby who won first prize at a local baby show.

Haymaking in the Brookside meadows involved part-timers partial to the doctor's cider. A flat field known as New Piece was bounded by the brook and the railway. Buckram bought himself a one-horse mowing machine and put Bob in between the shafts. A short blade, only two feet six inches long – smaller than the conventional Bramlett two horse machine – did a reasonable job on those seven acres.

The doctor's dray was a four wheeled railway type, yet lighter. There was a fore ladder and a rear ladder which fixed into the flat bed, making the vehicle half as long again. Dick, a black gelding, was between the dray shafts and Buckram was pitching the hay into the load while Moncrief loaded.

The doctor arrived after tea with Alec and Tom, who worked on a neighbouring farm. He wore a Panama hat in the hayfield, a kind of uniform of the gaffers of the mid-west, while the men wore battered straws the colour of egg yolks. Hats served two purposes; firstly as protection from the rays of the sun, and secondly to stop the hay seeds from falling down under the shirt collarband when the men got under the loaded dray to put the waggon rope on the hooks. The evening was hot and the grey-green hay smelt sweet. Alec and Tom had their Oxford shirt sleeves turned up to the elbows. They wore cord trousers with broadfall fronts. Tom looked at the doctor in his grey tight-fitting trousers, buttoned up boots and shirt. 'Beunt ya gwain to roll yer sleeves, Sir,' Alec said as he eyed the pearl cufflinks on the doctor's shirt. The doctor didn't answer but called Buckram and Moncrief, 'Now you boys, the men have arrived who know their job. One of you load the dray and Alec and Tom will give you a lesson in hay pitching.' Moncrief loaded. The doctor led Dick between the rows or valleys of hay and called 'Hold tight' to the young Robersons every time he moved on.

Buckram put Bob in the horse rake and raked up all the fallen hay behind the pitchers. The hay was being made safe for the winter, and the men and the Roberson boys made a rick next to Buckram's cowshed in the New Piece, a little hobby farm of the doctor's. They worked through the pleasant summer evening

until the evening star shone over the Cotswolds and the
company sat down under the partly made hay-rick
swilling the dust and pollen from their throats with the
doctor's cider from a stone jar. He totted out the juice of
last year's apples into cider horns, made from some
slaughtered beast and mottled in yellow and brown,
lovely cups, more right and fitting than crystal glass.
Then a little boy in cord knee breeches came running
down the cart track from Cinder Meadow. He carried a
note which he thrust into Edward Roberson's hand. It
read:

Dear Doctor,
Would you please come quickly to Paris on Bredon Hill,
my Missus has started labour.
Harry —

The doctor said to the boy, 'I'll be along presently,' then
turning to Alec and Tom said, 'No desperate hurry, she
'ull be a while yet. I've delivered all the other four.' The
doctor had another drink of cider before setting out on
his visit, working, as usual, at night.

Edward, beside being the owner of Rockland House,
had several more properties in the village. Pear Tree
Cottage, named after the giant pear tree in the garden
overlooking the road, was his surgery. This pear tree,
on Edward's instruction, had been grafted by Charlie
Hunting. It was a sight to behold in the autumn, for the
original perry tree now had a head of four different sorts
of fruit to enable the doctor to eat or cook pears from
summer until late autumn. One part of the tree grew
Jarjonelles, an early pear. Cheek by jowl to the Jarjonelles the sweet little Burgondy fruited alongside Clapps
Favourite and Pitmaston Duchess.
    The surgery itself had little of the modern fitments of
a man of medicine. A bare deal table, a brown crock

sink, but no tap; the standpipe on the roadside was his only water supply. Around the bare whitewashed walls the shelves were stocked with medicines. Large blue bottles marked 'Poison', measuring glasses, funnels, a pestle and mortar, in fact everything an early twentieth-century doctor stocked. Empty medicine bottles, white paper, sealing-wax, a steel-nibbed pen and a ink pot. Here he worked in a velvet jacket and smoking cap – a mystic, a wizard.

Sam, a farmer and innkeeper, passed by the surgery one day. He was on the School Board with the doctor. 'Sam,' the doctor called from his window. Sam walked into the surgery and sat down on a wooden chair beside the doctor, thinking that some business of the school was to be discussed. 'Have a drop of whisky,' the doctor offered.

'Ah, I will have one with you,' Sam replied. From the very top shelf Edward reached down a blue bottle marked 'Poison'. 'I'm not having any out of there,' Sam said in a state of panic.

'Why, I have to mark my whisky "Poison" or else other members of the family will drink it and leave none for me,' was the reply. After Edward had drunk some, Sam decided it was quite safe and joined the doctor in a drink out of the bottle marked 'Poison'.

The consulting room at Rockland House was to the right of the great oak door. It was an elegant room, furnished with his grandfather's suite, the polished mahogany table standing in the centre under an oil-burning chandelier. The fireplace was graced with *petit point* screens decorated with swans, kingfishers, woodpeckers and the like, and in the corner his leather sofa awaited patients. The tools of his trade were kept on shelves in a little anteroom at the back: forceps, scissors, bandages, tooth drawing instruments, all the first aid equipment of the day. Only medicines were kept in the surgery.

While hedge cutting one day, Ralph the carter ran a long blackthorn thorn into the middle of his hand. The hand turned septic, as often happened with blackthorn. After a restless night Ralph plucked up courage to see his doctor. 'It needs lancing, hold your hand out,' the doctor ordered and took a pair of scissors off the shelf in the anteroom, scissors which were anything but sharp. One or two attempts to cut the proud flesh failed until at last the great blister broke, the poison falling onto the polished mahogany table. 'Damn and blast,' the doctor shouted, and Ralph, with the pain relieved, felt it to be his fault. Muttering away about awkward folk who were careless enough to hurt their hands hedging, and plastering the wound with iodine then bandaging it up, the doctor sent yet another man of the soil on his way only to return again later in the year with a painful thumb nail where a piece of sprout stem had pushed back the quick and caused him pain. The doctor saved the nail and rubbed linseed oil into the sore, which, to Ralph's amazement, warted.

As the doctor treated his patients, took temperatures, examined tongues and eyelids for signs of illness, listened to the throbbing of hearts with his stethescope, Lavender stood in the road waiting for emergencies, an early ambulance of sorts. Lavender was harnessed every morning by Jeens, the doctor's manservant, and the trap stood all day long with Lavender between the shafts eating chopped chaffs, pulped mangolds and oats from a nosebag.

There were emergencies, fractures, etc. Grandad William Archer fell from a load of straw fracturing his skull as the muck cart passed Rockland House. With Grandad lying unconscious on a bed of straw, Edward Roberson followed the primitive ambulance to the cottage next to the White Hart pub and in the best possible way treated his patient.

Bessie, an elderly lady who lived outside the village at Land Close, had an accident during the night, after Lavender had been stabled. A hefty woman, Bessie had the misfortune to have the chamber-pot collapse under her weight and the pieces of crock cut her ample bottom badly. The doctor rode furiously down Pig Lane to Land Close on hearing the call for help. He dressed the wounds and stitched up the deep cut the broken chamber had given her.

A man for his time, Edward Roberson watched no clock but the sun and the moon – out with his gun in the day and visiting at all hours during the night. Seeing his patients at their worst had a certain common sense. He often operated on dining-tables. In one case in particular, a pregnancy in the fallopian tubes was terminated on a dining-table in one of the big houses. She was a poor girl who fell foul of a chauffeur.

Confinements were commonplace, but Edward would be there at any time, helped by Betsy Barnett who was a partly trained midwife and a layer-out of the dead. He had an inimitable humour. I think of Mrs J. who lived up Cottons Lane in a thatched cottage, the wife of a carter on what used to be Baldwyn's farm. She had three daughters and so badly wanted a son. When the point of no return arrived for the fourth time in her life, the doctor was delivering a straightforward birth. 'What is it Doctor?' she anxiously asked.

'Wait a bit Ellen, a little longer. Ah, it's another girl.'

Ellen burst into tears sobbing her heart out and crying, 'Doctor, I did so much want a boy.' It was the doctor's humour that poured oil on the troubled waters of the carter's wife. He knew Ellen and spoke to her not as some out-of-touch medico, but as a friend, a village anchor, and a man who understood the small world under the hill. 'It's no good Ellen, not your fault at all, but Old Jack can't get you a baby with a spout on. Perhaps you ought to try a different horse.' Here was language that the carter's wife understood; kind in a way, the doctor trying to make light of Ellen's plight. Her tears dried and she laughed on her straw mattress under the thatch as the light shone again through the dormer window under the beams.

Mildred, a farmer's widow, had many admirers. She was an Elizabeth Taylor of the twenties. Pretty, coy, painted; drove a fast cob in her governess car. The sight of her driving the eleven miles to Cheltenham, the rubber tyred car rocking its way down the village street, the cane whip waving from its pipe-like holder on the mudguard, and Mildred, dressed in one of Cavendish House's latest creations, made working men lean on their hoes and wipe the sweat from their brows, a picture of rural beauty. Her suitors ranged between a farmer from across the vale; a gentleman who had a music shop in town and ran steamers on the river Avon; a shoemaker, ex-army, who became very jealous of the rest; and a man of independent means named William who rode a green Sunbeam bicycle. William became ill and visited his good friend Doctor Roberson in the consulting room one evening. Edward did the usual tests with stethescope and thermometer, and, as William lay stripped on the sofa, he awaited the doctor's diagnosis. 'Well Bill, I must tell you that you are overdoing your nature with Mildred. Take it easy boy.' How much leg-pull, how much humour were in Edward's words is left to the imagination. Maybe Edward was a little jealous of William; it's hard to know, for the incidents in the doctor's early life give the impression that he was quite a judge of the ladies.

The doctor, it's quite evident, was always concerned for the poor. They trusted him when their babies were born. There was a case of a premature birth when the child was thought to be dead; this was at a time before intensive care and incubators. The doctor worked on the child and it began to breathe and cry. He dabbed a little brandy on its lips. It lived and as the boy grew to manhood, he called it the miracle baby.

Edward Roberson sought no reward for the long hours he spent in all winds and weathers at night time, while the village lay sleeping on their matresses made from the breast feathers of the white Wyandotte and the old English game fowl. Honour, the widow of a railway ganger, lay between life and death fighting pneumonia. It was late on a Sunday night when the doctor called.

'No crisis, yet, but she needs poulticing,' he told Tom, her son. 'And I'm run out of linseed meal.' He looked gravely at Honour, then at Tom, fearing the worst. Tom said, 'Doctor, there's plenty of linseed over in the barn which I use for the calves, but it's not been ground into meal.'

'Damn it, we can grind it can't we,' the doctor replied, adding, 'Come on, lets grind some.'

Tom lit a hurricane lamp and together they went to the Rushton Hornsby oil engine in the barn. Tom pumped away at the blow lamp under the vapourizer and then lit it. The blue flame roared away changing the vapourizer from a cold red tube four inches in diameter and nine inches long to white-hot. Tom gave the intake valve a few pumps and injected paraffin oil into the white-hot vapourizer. Two big flywheels stood at each end of the axle. A leather driving belt was then put on the pulley wheel beside the one flywheel and fixed on the pulley of the corn mill. 'Hold the lantern please Doctor, and I'll start the engine.' Tom gave a strong pull on the wheel and the engine coughed. He pulled it over compression, the engine turned, turning with it the false pulley on the mill. With another leaver Tom switched the driving belt from the loose pulley into the fast driving pulley on the mill. The mill

The Close, Ashton-under-Hill

Doctor Roberson in his trap at Ashton Cross

Amy with Buckram and Moncrief

turned and in the lantern light the barn vibrated to the power of the engine.

From the engine house the two men walked through the barn door and Tom took a sack of linseed, pouring some into a bushel measure. He set the mill so that the grist would be fine and poured the linseed into the hopper. Another bushel measure under the mill filled slowly with meal. 'How much do you want Doctor?' Tom shouted above the noise of the machinery.

'Do half a hundredweight Tom, there's a hell of a lot of flu about and other people will go down with it and need poulticing.'

In the barn several barrels of cider stood trammed under the wall. One had a wooden tap in it and a tub underneath. 'Fancy a drop a cider Doctor?' Tom said.

'Ah, but let's poultice your mother. Fill a gallon costrel barrel and bring it along with the meal.'

Tom carried the meal for the poultice and the doctor carried the gallon of cider. Tom's wife sat by her mother-in-law waiting for the men to return. She had a kettle of water boiling on the kitchen range and the doctor soon applied the hot linseed poultice made from the meal and the hot water. Honour slept noisily, comforted by the heat from the poultice. 'She will need another poultice in about a couple of hours,' the doctor said to Tom and his wife.

'A drop of cider Doctor?' Tom asked Edward Roberson.

Tom's wife put two wooden armchairs on each side of the range and poured out two mugs of cider for the men. Strange companions – one a doctor and the other a cowman, but there was a bond between a village professional and a worker of the land. They talked the rest of the night away. Tom talked of his basic veterinary skills with horses and cows while the doctor explained how that once the crisis passed in cases of pneumonia the high temperature fell and the danger was over.

'Bad job about the young Barnett boy who died after he sowed the basic slag on Ten Acre Piece,' Tom said as he sipped cider from his mug.

'Ah, if only the farmer had given him a good allowance of cider when he sowed the slag he would have been with us today. You see, slag is fine, it gets on the lungs and the cider would have got rid of the phlegm on his chest,' replied the doctor.

Two hours had passed, the doctor put another poultice on Honour's chest. She was awake and more comfortable. 'I'll stay another two hours, Tom, and poultice her again, then it won't be long until morning. These small hours are the worst for pneumonia patients.'

Honour got better and lived until she was eighty-five, saved by an oil engine and the bedside manner of Edward Roberson.

# THE ROBERSONS AND BREDON HILL

The Roberson family had a great affinity with Bredon Hill. It was their playground, their vantage point. At times they slept under the moon and stars on Bredon. Thomas Packer of Cheltenham, author of *Around Bredon Hill*, and Doctor Roberson were great friends. When they started the Cirencester and Tewkesbury Conservative Sick and Dividend Society Thomas Packer brought a lot of supporters from Cheltenham in horsedrawn carriages every Club Day. Club Day was Trinity Monday. All work stopped that day and the Ashton folk made merry after the church service in the morning. The doctor presided at the Club Feast and Moncrief recalled to me that when the Cheltenham folk were ready to return home in the evening the grand carriages pulled by sleek horses and decorated with blue Tory ribbons, were lined up outside Rockland House. The horses were impatient to go those eleven miles to Cheltenham, and the drivers held them as they scorted their hooves on the limestone road ('scorted', a good word for an impatient scuffling).

The Robersons often picnicked on Bredon Hill. Many's the time I've seen the girls carrying the kettle of water from Paris Springs on the hill to the Cuckoo Pen. Here an outcrop of stone lay just below the pen of beech trees – a circle of ancient trees on the high ground of Little Hill. At this outcrop, loose stones were placed to form a square for the fire. Wood abounded on Little Hill. The red colour left by the fire on the stones would tell the tale of a recent picnic. Barbara would be in charge of the fire, and Amy, another of the doctor's daughters, laid the tea cloth on the close rabbit-cropped turf. No teapot was needed. The tea was added to the kettle after the water had boiled. By this method they brewed a good cup of tea, adding the rich milk from Buckram's Devon cows to the cup.

The doctor encouraged his family to lead an outdoor life. They spent the autumn days blackberrying, using the fruit for jam-making and for selling at the market. Here was food for free, together with the mushrooms which grew in abundance on Ashton Wood plain.

# WILLIAM ARCHER AND
# MARY ANN ARCHER

My grandfather, William Archer, worked part-time for
Squire Baldwyn and part-time on his smallholding.
The Baldwyn ricks were being threshed at Middle
Farm, where the squire's bailiff lived. William was
loading straw into a farm waggon. His load was almost
finished. The straw was in boltins – trusses of straw
tied with a straw bond. Men stood at the back of the
thresher and tied these boltins and pitched them to
William. The foreladder of the waggon broke and
William fell on to the stone floor of the rickyard where
he lay unconscious with a fractured skull.

Baldwyn's men lifted him on to some straw on the
floor of a muck cart. With one of the men leading the
horse, the cart, a very cruel ambulance, conveyed
William to his cottage half a mile away over a rough
village lane. Dr Roberson came straight away and
prescribed the only treatment he knew at that time –
cold compresses on his brow. William lay unconscious
for days and every day the doctor came. He ordered ice
from the fish shop in Evesham to make the ice packs
for William's fevered head.

William belonged to the Cirencester and Tewkesbury Sick and Dividend Society. They paid his wife
Mary Ann a few shillings a week and also paid the
doctor; he was their surgeon. Eventually William
Archer recovered, or partly recovered, for he was
never the same after the accident. He never worked for
the squire again, but he did manage his smallholding.
The skull fracture resulted in him being temperamen-
tal and difficult. Doctor Roberson saved his life, but
had not the know-how in the nineteenth-century that

we have today. Today William would have been treated in hospital.

Some years after Grandad's death in 1900, Grandmother fell and fractured her femur. She was a big woman like all the Archers of that day. Grandmother Mary Ann had been ill for a little while before the fall and my cousin Nellie Breeze was looking after her with Ethel Whittle. These two girls were friends and they wanted to go to Dumbleton Flower Show together. Mary Ann told them she would be alright, but while they were away she had the accident.

Again Doctor Edward Roberson was called. He put her leg in splints and called every two days to try to set it. Grandmother hung on to the head of her brass bedstead and twisted the bed end as she writhed in pain. The doctor tried to get her on her feet again, but it was a losing battle, partly because of her great weight. When it became obvious that the doctor would not succeed, Dad told him, 'No more doctor. Leave her, she has suffered enough pain.' She died in 1910.

# DOCTOR ROBERSON AS A VILLAGE NOTARY

A patient at Conderton, affectionately known as Bumper because of his fast short bowling at cricket, called on the doctor. Bumper had a rash. He was a confirmed bachelor. The doctor examined him and could not give an opinion about the itchy condition of his skin. He looked sternly at Bumper and said, 'You haven't been messing about the pea picking women have you?' The Doctor treated him with soft soap and cleared the rash.

Village folk are slow to accept 'outsiders', but when I was a boy Dr Roberson was part of the village scene.

However, he was never accepted by the Baldwyn family. He was often irritated by the naivety of his fellow members of the Parish Council, but worse was to come.

Retired people from Birmingham, Liverpool and London were finding a peaceful life under Bredon Hill. Two of them were elected to the Parish Council; an artist from Liverpool and an engineer from Birmingham. They had great ideas about altering the life-style of the village. They proposed a scheme to put a piped water supply into every house. This was going to bump up the rates. At a Parish Meeting Doctor Roberson and a Mr Baldwyn did join forces to veto the scheme. A recent arrival in the village, a gentleman's gardener, spoke at length at this meeting. An old market gardener rose to his feet – six feet of corduroy and hobnails. 'Thee sit down, thee hasn't been in the village long enough to get your seat warm.' These words from Alf about flattened the gentleman's gardener. The Doctor ruled O.K.

At the doctor's surgery things were primitive. He had to carry the water to mix his medicines from a roadside standpipe – I've seen him standing there with a bucket under the tap waiting for it to fill. He often had to wait a long time, for the pressure of the water outside Rockland House was low. Rockland House was high up the village street, and if folk were drawing water lower down the village, the doctor's supply was reduced to a trickle. Doctor Roberson can be admired for voting against the scheme for a new water supply. He had the good of the farm labourers at heart.

Inside his surgery the doctor had a brown crock sink which drained into the roadside ditch. No tap, but a bucket of water and a jug. It has been said that the doctor only had two kinds of medicine, one for over-indulgence at the Club Feast and Christmas and another for flu. He once sent Dad's partner a bill for forty pounds, a lot of money in the 1920s. When he was told that the bill was excessive the doctor replied, 'It's no good me sending bills to those folk who haven't got the money, and besides, the drugs I've given your daughter are devilishly expensive.'

Mrs Lippet who did his washing and also did ours used to tell a tale about the doctor's shirts. She said that he cut the tail off his shirts for bandages. I wonder. Nothing would surprise me. 'Nair a bit of tail on any of his shirts, Master,' she told Dad. There would be emergencies, but a shirt tail for bandages?

Oh yes, Mr Hughes the artist looked smart in his nicely cut fawn suit and trilby hat as he came down the street. Harold Wigley on his way to church in his Sunday best did make some of the farm workers in cottage gardens drinking cider touch their caps as he passed. But the doctor looked different; he commanded respect. He was a handsome man even in old age. No wonder he had bowled so many maidens over with his charm. His smart appearance seemed to give confidence to his patients.

It must be admitted that the way he dressed in the 1920s was definitely Victorian, early Victorian. He wore a box hat, a cross between a top hat and a bowler. These were in vogue at the turn of the century. Above his closely cropped beard and moustache his cheeks were rosy. His outdoor life with his gun had given him the look of a farmer, but his dress while on his rounds was that of a city gentleman. He wore a long black jacket with four cloth-covered buttons, a white shirt with a starched 'Come to Jesus' collar (and no shirt tail?), and a bright red cravat with a golden tie-pin. His black waistcoat was chained from buttonhole to pocket by a golden Albert, a chain hung with sovereigns. The doctor's pinstriped black and white trousers clipped him below the knee, and were shaped narrow to the ankle. His shoes were what some folk call high lows – they were neither boots nor shoes. They were black leather with elastic at the side which dispensed with the usual laces. Around his ankles in wintertime he wore spats of a felt material. On his rounds in the village he carried a Gladstone bag and he walked with a silver-mounted walking-stick. The man was impressive, he scared me, but how the old folk loved him.

# THE DOCTOR AND POLITICS

Dr Roberson was a nominal Tory. He supported Mr Hicks Beach, M.P. for Cheltenham, in an election campaign before the Great War. The doctor was not in his constituency but he had lots of connections in Cheltenham.

Since its inception late in the nineteenth century, Ashton Club was a Conservative organisation. In fact its full title was the Cirencester and Tewkesbury Conservative Sick and Dividend Society. Dr Packer, who founded the Club, was also, like Roberson, a churchman. There is a tablet in the parish church at Cheltenham in memory of this man, and his book, *Around Bredon Hill*, was considered a classic in local topography.

Roberson, the ardent Tory, a man of the establishment, did lose his zest for their cause in later life. One reason for this was that the doctor felt that the way the labouring folk were treated was far from fair. The Poor Law, with a Baldwyn as the Guardian, was insensitive to the needs of the aged and infirm. Another reason was that the Baldwyns were rank Tories, and any connection with the Baldwyns was like a red rag to a bull for Edward Roberson.

Pedlar, a small market gardener and fruit grower, and a highly respected employer, hated the Baldwyns and hated the family who had bought Baldwyn land. A sort of conspiracy developed between Pedlar and the doctor. Although great opposites in most things, they had one thing in common – they were trying to better the lot of the working man. To say Pedlar was a Socialist would be putting it mildly. He was left of left; he was working for the revolution as had recently been witnessed in Russia. The nearest thing that Pedlar could get to his ideas was to form a local branch of the Labour Party. Tustin lived opposite the Star Inn and was always eager to earn a shilling. He put his front room at the disposal of the local Labour Party for a rent of half a crown. It was here in this bare room where cardboard replaced glass window panes and the age-old white geraniums stood on the sill, that the Party was formed.

Tustin was joined by Ern, Harry, Sapper and Charlie. The doctor supported the group with a handsome cheque. His theory was to get Pedlar and Harry as a driving force in the village to join him on the Parish Council and oppose the Baldwyns and their friends. Pedlar's son, Darwin, had been to Ruskin College, Oxford and gave lectures in Tustin's cottage on the Marxist doctrine. The group at Tustin's cottage had a visit from the Labour Party's prospective candidate, a Mr Robbins. The Tories said, 'Cock Robin won't winter it,' but the following May he stood as the candidate. Robbins was not elected but he didn't lose his deposit. Neither Pedlar nor Harry ever joined the doctor on the Parish Council but they did make themselves heard at the parish meetings.

# THE DOCTOR'S MEDICINE

Old villagers who were patients of Dr Roberson were adamant that his prescriptions and patient care cured them of many serious illnesses. 'A clever man', some said. 'A long headed man', others said. I don't think he was a genius, but a good practitioner in his time. His time was past when I knew him. He had not kept up with the more modern approach to medicine.

He had one, I think, quite unique trait. He was a good visitor because he came at night. When he sat at the bedside of some old villager and talked, that did tend towards healing. It's true he talked even longer through the night, if the man's wife was liberal with her home-made wine.

I've seen the doctor often at night in the village. To be more precise, I've seen a man in black hurrying to a patient, holding in his hand a jam jar with a short candle glowing like a glow-worm. In his other hand he held his Gladstone bag with all the mysteries of his profession. He muttered to himself as he walked. His soft leather boots made little noise; they squeaked their way over the rough limestone lane. His day, or should I say his night, had only just begun. I would stand on the grass verge as he passed. He was the village oracle – magic. In the dim light of his candle I'd sometimes see Sailor following his master. It was always said in the village that even in a howling gale his candle never went out. That bothered me as a boy and made me wonder whether this man was a witch-doctor.

There was something about the doctor's medicine which relieved symptoms even if it didn't cure the patient. Men on the land would say, 'I've been pretty middling lately. I'll have to get another bottle of the doctor's jalap.' What jalap did I can't imagine, but that bottle of medicine would be considered a lifeline. The cloudy mixture was dispensed in bottles wrapped in white paper and sealed with sealing-wax. The doctor emphasized the importance of giving the bottle a thundering good shake before drinking the mixture. The drugs were camouflaged by the taste of pepper-mint or ginger.

In the 1920s a lady came to the village from Scotland and stayed with relatives in a house belonging to Dr Roberson. She was a little woman, middle-aged, and a spinster. It was quite evident that this lady came from a family of a higher class than the run of the mill villagers. Her dress was of the finest materials and well cut. She went regularly to St Barbara's church and it was no secret that the ten shilling note on the collection plate was from her. Her name was Wilhelmina. Every morning she walked down to the railway station and caught the 8.50 train to Evesham, sometimes returning on the four o'clock train. At the surgery the doctor prescribed medicine for her nerves. There was a mystery about Wilhelmina – it was said that she had been jilted by a Scottish Lord. At that time neither the Plough and Harrow nor the Star Inn had a wine and spirit licence; they were cider and ale houses. Wilhelmina drank spirits. She drank much too much. The spirits came by train to the station – stone jars of gin, etc.

Often Wilhelmina would be drunk in the doctor's surgery. He tried talking to her, and gave her medicine which he said would stem her craving for drink. The fact was that Wilhelmina was very lonely. She paid handsomely for her keep, but apart from church on Sunday, her time was spent alone.

The doctor made an appointment for her to see a specialist in Cheltenham and they went together to his grand house in Royal Crescent. The specialist suggested that Wilhelmina should have a few weeks in a nursing home. Dr Roberson discussed this proposition with her over lunch at The Plough Hotel, but she insisted, 'I'll stay as your patient Edward, I have faith in you alone.' He could not persuade her to go, and after all, the bills she paid him for treatment were as regular as a farmer's monthly milk cheque.

After Christmas the snow melted and the river Avon was in flood. Even the little Carrants Brook flowed over the meadows. Blenheim, Baldwyn's cowman, kept the milking herd in Cinder Meadow. Twice a day he drove the cows from the field by the railway line to the cowyard at Holloway Farm. Early one morning he and the herd came through Little Piece. When they reached the pool Blenheim's dog barked persistently. 'What is it Rosie; 'tis only a moorhen,' Blenheim said to his dog. On looking closely into the pool in the half moonlight the cowman could see a body, a woman's body. Blenheim caught hold of her coat collar and dragged the body to the bank. Leaving the cows, Blenheim rushed to Rockland House. Everything was quiet in the early morning, and there was no answer when he banged on the front door. The cowman threw pebbles against the doctor's bedroom window. Edward Roberson appeared and called out, 'What's going on? I'll get the gun to you, whoever you are.'

Blenheim answered, ''Tis only me Doctor. I've found a drowned woman in Little Piece pond.'

It was unusual for Doctor Roberson to be up and about at six o'clock in the morning. He dressed and accompanied Blenheim to Little Piece pond. 'She's dead and it's Wilhelmina. Fetch the policeman and someone to help carry her. I'll stay here,' he said.

The police arrived. Blenheim and Jim, Baldwyn's carter, carried the little woman's body to Rockland House on a hurdle. Her cousin came, an old lady very distressed. 'Leave the body in my library, we don't want to upset the relatives', the doctor said to the police officer, adding, 'There will have to be an inquest.'

Dad was on the jury at the inquest in Rockland House. The doctor told the jury and the coroner that Wilhelmina was an alcoholic, an inebriate woman. Blenheim gave evidence of finding the body in the pool, giving his uncalled-for assessment of the case: 'Her must have gone off her yud.' A note was found in the bedroom where she stayed at her relatives' house.

They found her will, in which she left her money and effects to the relatives, all except her gold watch and chain. This was left to Doctor Roberson for his kindness.

The pond where Wilhelmina drowned has now been filled in and Little Piece is a cricket ground. The pavillion is built almost on the site of the pond.

# THE DOCTOR AND THE CHURCH

Edward Roberson took a keen interest in the life of St Barbara's church, being appointed People's Warden soon after he came to the village. He served under Revd John Gough, a high churchman and a scholar, the Vicar's Warden being David Drinkwater, the last of a line of Drinkwaters who had served the village for centuries. David, a yeoman farmer and a haulier, kept a team of horses up Cottons Lane and hauled stones off Bredon Hill to maintain roads.

The whole of the church building spoke of the Baldwyn family. Tablets of stone in the walls were inscribed with the names of past generations – of Thomas, Bernard, William, and Henry – while under-foot the floor was covered with Baldwyn memorials. In later years, when the remains of the dead were no longer buried under the church floor, the Baldwyn vault was built under the tower, and it was here that Amy's father and her brother who died at school were laid to rest.

Amy played the organ on Sunday nights. She had a bent for music. Bunch, her sister, was not quite such a genius on the keyboard, but her rendering of 'The Funeral March' had to be heard to be believed, for every timber, every pane of glass, clear or stained, resonated when she pulled out the stops and thundered the bass notes.

The doctor, as People's Warden, was also treasurer of the church and he alone took up the collection, missing no one with the plate. After the service he funnelled the silver and copper coins into his trouser pocket and secured them in the safe at Rockland House.

John Clements had been Parish Clerk until his death in old age. He was a bespoke tailor, a maker of breeches for the farmers and costumes for the ladies. He was succeeded by his son-in-law, Charlie, as Parish Clerk and Sexton. Charlie was a hurdlemaker and was nicknamed Stocky. He could remember seeing John Clements sitting under the pulpit when the village orchestra made a kind of music to accompany the psalms and hymns before the organ was installed.

Stocky was steeped in the ways of High Church under Revd Gough. His rendering of 'Armen' with a gutteral Gloucestershire accent reverberated under the arched roof. Sometimes he put an extra answer into Revd Gough's intonations. Never was a worshipper able to forget that Stocky was Clerk. His game leg restricted him a little as he limped like a peewit feigning injury when protecting its young, but the short ash plant, a knobbed walking stick, helped him around the building – it was also useful to whack any mischievous choirboy in the vestry.

Stocky's inimitable way of dousing candles was noticeable to visitors, but accepted as part of the ritual by the villagers. He blew them out one by one with noisy puffs, like an engine letting off steam on threshing days. The doctor told him to restrain himself, but to no avail.

When Revd Gough died and Revd Margetts took over the living, Stocky didn't approve of the new parson. He didn't like his habit of shaking hands with his parishoners as they left the church, and described him as 'Low Chapel'. Revd Margetts was appalled to hear that Stocky and Revd Gough had refused to bury an unbaptised infant, but he had no success in restraining Stocky with his loud 'Armens'.

It was Stocky who tolled the bell announcing a funeral in the village. He limped in front of the funeral procession, next to the vicar, as the bier borrowed from the next village creaked its way down the rough village street, the bearers wearing black-turned-green suits and shallow ancient bowler hats. 'Ashes to ashes, dust to dust', the vicar said at the graveside, as Stocky plonked lumps of clay into the grave, which resounded on the coffin lid. Margetts had told him to riddle some fine soil for the purpose, but to no avail. Before the mourners had had time to depart the sexton was shovelling the clay back into the grave.

Doctor Roberson never missed a funeral if he could help it, but if he was called away to an emergency, David Drinkwater took over. The doctor was pleased with Revd Margetts, who was a humble man. Gough had constituted a threat to the man who had married into the Baldwyn clan, which to Gough was sacrosant.

The doctor had brought many into the world and had seen many cross over Jordan, and he, as Church Warden, instigated the extension of the churchyard.

# THE DOCTOR AND THE SCHOOL

The village school was a church school, built in the 1870s. Years before its opening, Archdeacon Timbrell had taught a few of the sons and daughters of the labourers in the church vestry, then Revd Joseph Harrison became vicar on Timbrell's death and carried on teaching both on weekdays and at Sunday school. Harrison was a friend of the poor, a good shepherd, but often the worse for drink. As a boy, my Uncle Jim was always pleased when the vicar had taken too much whisky, for then lessons were short and the genial parish priest closed with his well known words, 'Don't do as I do, but do as I tell you.'

Doctor Edward Roberson became Chairman of the Village School Board soon after he came to the village and Revd Gough had taken Harrison's place as vicar. Together they went almost daily to the little school, Gough trying to instil the creed and ordinance of the Church of England, while Edward tested them on arithmetic. In Revd Margetts' time as vicar, a Mr Somerville was appointed schoolmaster. He, a handsome bachelor, soon had the bigger girls swooning after him. They were loth to go home in the evening.

Doctor Roberson kept everything at that little nineteenth-century school very much in order. While Revd Margetts tutored the pupils in the Creed, Doctor Roberson was a regular visitor, teaching and questioning the top class on general knowledge. He knew more of the world than a whole bevy of villagers together. His father had been a rector, his one brother a sea captain, another a lawyer, while his grandfather had been Town Clerk of Oxford. He was steeped in professionalism, and many village lads and lassies had a lifelong benefit from Edward, Mr Somerville and Revd Margetts. Edward also kept a keen eye on the health of the pupils at the little church school.

During one hard winter Edward made it a practice, much against his life-style of late rising, to be at the school promptly at the nine o'clock opening time. Armed with a thermometer he took the temperature and, turning to the headteacher, pronounced his finding. 'Forty degrees,' he said sharply. 'Alter the timetable Somerville, I don't want half these children at home with flu, and only me to look after them.' Somerville, a young man, wondered just what the doctor would order. They studied the thermometer together, then the doctor said, 'Today you will keep your pupils warm by alternating the time with singing and physical exercises.' So the books stayed in the cupboard, the pens and pencils on the desks, Amy came and played the piano and the pupils sang anything from 'The British Grenadiers' to 'Tom Bowling'. A wise move on Edward's part. He knew every child, every parent and every grandparent.

That winter was particularly severe, the hardest since 1898 when Jim Vale told me of sixteen weeks frost in February. 'What a long February,' I said.

'Oi, me and thee Uncle Jim walked around Bredon Hill at Christmas. He played the melodian and I sang the carols, then we bought a lot of herrings and sold them around the villages. No work, no pay.'

The doctor had treated Grandfather for rheumatism caused by getting wet through while laying the drain pipes to drain Cinder Meadow and then walking home, his corduroy trousers freezing on his legs in the evening frost. This was at a time before Wellington boots had been invented.

One may say that forty degrees in a school classroom is bleak, but worse to come. One morning at nine o'clock Edward's thermometer registered thirty-two degrees. 'That's freezing, Somerville. Close the school; send them home; let them go hunting or playing hare and hounds on Bredon Hill. I won't be responsible as Chairman of the Board for these children staying here when my thermometer registers freezing.' So the boys and girls went home. When Revd Margetts arrived he joined the doctor for a whisky at Rockland House.

# THE DOCTOR ON THE MEDICAL BOARD, THE COUNCIL AND THE BENCH

Soon after the outbreak of the 1914 war, when men were conscripted for the forces, Edward Roberson became a member of the Medical Board. Young men of the village who belonged to the Sick and Dividend Society were well known to the doctor. He had a pretty good inkling who would make a soldier. Cousin George, who had hammer toes, was rejected and as a 'Grade C' man was told to continue working on the land with Dad's horses. The doctor was emphatic that he was not military material. Another member of the board questioned George asking him how he managed to walk on the furrowed land, and got the reply that he hung on to the plough or any implement he worked with.

In wartime there have been many young men anxious to serve their country who, if deemed unfit, are disappointed. Others have 'dodged the column', or 'swung the leg'. One of the doctor's patients was ill all through the war. It may have been psychosomatic, who knows, but Edward was instrumental in getting him out of war service. I remember one such man, a man who could be both comical and sarcastic. During the 1939 war Blenheim was propelling himself past my rickyard as best he could on his arthritic legs and with the aid of an ash plant. He was doing his bit on the land, digging out a ditch. A man who had escaped war service during the First World War drew his bike up alongside Blenheim.

'Had your calling up papers yet, Blenheim?' he asked.

'Papers, papers,' Blenheim replied, 'Who was it who had the rheumatic and bellyache all through the last war and the doctor got him out of the army, then he never voted for him at the election.' Powerful stuff from Blenheim, right on target.

As Chairman of the District Council Edward served the village and district impartially and well, but when he became deaf he had difficulty. Being a little man, he always sat on the minute book to give him a bit more height. It is difficult for a man so hard of hearing to keep up with the constant flow of proposals and secondings of the Council members. The doctor lost track of the meeting. 'Will someone propose the motion?' Edward called from the Chair. 'It's been proposed and seconded, Doctor. Will you put it to the meeting?' the Clerk shouted into Edward's cupped ear. The time came when because of his deafness the doctor had to resign from the council.

He was an early conservationist, preferring things in the village to stay as they were and had been when the Baldwyns were squires. The hill, the fruit trees, the hawthorn hedges, were sacred to him. A problem arose when the council surveyor proposed that the stream which ran from the spring water on the hill through Shaw Green and followed the roadside in front of Rockland House should be piped. It was a pretty stream, crossed by little stone-built causeways or bridges to the gateways of the cottages. Edward was strongly against such an intrusion, despite the fact that if the stream was piped the road could be widened.

This was one of his last fights on the council. He liked to see and hear the stream from Rockland House. Some said he was against the scheme because his little flock of Khaki Campbell ducks swam in the stream and sometimes laid their eggs in the bottom of the sparkling spring water. It may have had a bearing on his judgement, who knows. He lost his fight. The stream was piped, and Bourton-on-the-Water in miniature was lost for ever.

The doctor was a J.P., and always showed compassion for the poor when they came to the Petty Sessions charged with poaching rabbits on the hill. There was a sympathy between them, maybe prompted by his wife, for in later years she mellowed him. Villagers who helped him with his haymaking or fencing and hedging were welcome to get rabbits with their ferrets from the warrens under the gorse on his hill. Farmers who worked horses with sore shoulders or didn't put the skid pan under the waggon wheel when they locked the wheel coming down the street were not treated so sympathetically. 'They should know better,' he said.

# THE DOCTOR'S CHILDREN

## MARY

Mrs Amy Roberson's death in middle age was a great blow to her husband. She had, despite indifferent health, steered the Roberson ship as a young mother. Mary, the eldest child, had always accompanied her mother on visits to friends, and on shopping trips by train to Cheltenham. On her mother's death Mary was stunned to such an extent that she never went out of doors in the daytime. Happy she was on Bredon Hill under the moon. She would walk long distances during the night but the prospect of facing villagers in the daylight without the support of her mother was too much for her. So for nearly sixty-five years Mary has lived in Rockland House, a recluse by day, yet keeping in touch with the outside world by nightly visits to family and friends. No doubt she found comfort in her constant trek across those grassy paths to Grafton to

Barbara, Mary, Amy and Buckram

Barbara and Amy with
Sailor and Dash

Moncrief at Ashton
School

spend the dark hours with her youngest sister, Ruth, known as Cissy.

Mary and her brother, Moncrief, used to pick plums for me on the slopes of Bredon Hill in the moonlight. In the morning I would find a nicely written note tucked under the front door of my farmhouse. The note was to say how many chips of fruit they had picked. Each chip basket held twelve pounds and they would be stacked under a tarpaulin sheet in the hedge bottom.

I had some laying hens in the next field on stubble and it was late when I went there to shut the henhouse up safe from the fox. Silhouetted against the night sky Moncrief's form made a picture as he picked plums from a short ladder. Mary was picking fruit from the lower branches of the tree. The moon had risen over the Cotswold edge and while most folk were by the fireside, these two good people picked my plums.

That winter as I motored along the road from Grafton, Mary, dressed in her usual black, was returning late from her sister's farm. Feeling that the quite elderly lady was at risk from traffic dressed in black on a black, dark night, I bought her a torch and left it at Rockland House. Her lovely letter of thanks made it worthwhile, for I had told Mary that her life was still precious to us all. Eccentric, yes, but a kind, gentle lady unnoticed by many because she kept such odd hours. The Robersons were never nine-'til-five people.

Mary once told me of her passion for horse racing and how she got such pleasure in studying form in the paper and placing her bets with a Cheltenham book-maker. I gather the transactions would have been through the post. She also used to send away for quite expensive clothes. No one saw her in the dresses she wore in Rockland House, but she, by wearing beautiful things, with only the mirror to say how lovely, gained something intangible, an independence she cherished.

As I write, Mary still lives her life as a hermit. At ninety she is the last of the doctor's children to survive.


## AMY

I didn't know Amy, the doctor's daughter, very well, but do recall how smart and upright a lady she was. She inherited the Baldwyn presence and her father's personality. Amy was away from Rockland House for some time, working as a receptionist at a doctor's practice in the Cotswolds. She married Fred Kempton, who had been a banker but had come to live in the country because of failing health. In fact, both Fred and Amy were delicate and decided to live on the slopes of Bredon near the fruit plantation Fred was working. A prefabricated bungalow was erected just before the wedding on what was known as the Doctor's Hill. The doctor in fact owned both the hill and the fruit plantation. My friend Len Whittle worked for Fred and between them they built the bungalow, later known as Coney Hill.

I remember Fred and Amy walking past our house on their way to the railway station, Fred dressed in tweeds, already going bald and slightly bent beside his bride. She could not go unnoticed by the rural men and women. Amy had dignity, more dignity than her sisters, a charming lady who died too soon; and so, unhappily, did Fred. They were middle class folk, yet of the people, a couple who enjoyed their cell on Bredon among the gorse, the rabbits and blackberries. The bungalow had no electricity, and water had to be carried from a standpipe near Box Cottage. Fred, with horse and trap, took the produce of the fruit plantation to market. He had a good old-fashioned gardener to help him in Leonard. Making money was not the chief object. The whole pattern of life revolved around the free pure air of Bredon, and the good honest mate in Amy.

Leonard Whittle added extra spice to their lives with his tales of the old squire, and of how, as a young chap, he had been double-crossed by a farmer who had promised that if Len and some other young men would vote for him in the elections for the district council, they could clear an area of scrub land and use it for allotments. 'How we were deceived,' Leonard said. The farmer took back the land when they had cleaned it, because he failed at the election. It is known to this day as The Promised Land.

One can only hope that Fred Kempton's decision to give up his city job and grow fruit on Bredon Hill with Amy at his side may have lenghthened his life a little. The marriage was a loving one, and Fred and Amy made a little history at Coney Hill on Bredon's slopes.

## BARBARA

I knew the doctor's third daughter, Barbara, well. No doubt she was so-named because the parish church was dedicated to St Barbara. Her mother would have made sure that one of her daughters took the name of her beloved church.

This daughter kept the village shop for many years, a cute little cottage shop next to the doctor's surgery. Here under the enormous pear tree, Barbara Roberson sold things so diverse as paraffin and custard powder. Behind the counter, where a simple bacon slicer would cut bacon of a more reasonable thickness than the modern machines, Barbara stood surrounded by all the groceries, the candles, the cigarettes and tobacco. She was an elegant lady with glasses who looked more like a schoolmarm than a shopkeeper.

In those far-off days only four delivery vans came to the village: one delivering Lyons tea; a chain-driven Trojan carrying Brooke Bond tea; Wards of Evesham delivering paraffin; and a green van with the legend D.C.L. on its side came with yeast for Mr Clements the baker. All the other groceries for Barbara's shop came by horse and dray from Tewkesbury. The Robersons were essentially Gloucestershire people who chose to deal with Tewkesbury rather than Evesham.

It's anyone's guess if Barbara made a living at the shop. She had a business ability but was kind-hearted to the poor. Her hours were long and, true to family tradition, she worked into the night being often still open near midnight. The oil lamp burned, the oil stove warmed the late shoppers, and Buckram, her brother, would impishly call very late and announce in a deep bass voice, 'Miss Roberson, can I have a packet of Woodbines and a box of matches?'

Barbara lived at Rockland House and used the cottage purely as a shop. The little window lit by a flickering oil lamp would be tastefully dressed for Christmas with white mesh Christmas stockings, pink sugar mice, and an almost life-size dummy of Santa Claus peeping through the window.

One Christmas at Rockland House, Albert the houseboy, who always lit the doctor's pipe with a spill, set fire to the old man's beard by accident, and then left the tap running on the cider barrel in the cellar as he brought jugs of the amber juice to the dining-room. The doctor was missing after supper, much to the consternation of the family, for several times that winter he had suffered heart attacks. On his return, Moncrief said, 'Where have you been Dad?'

'Just to mark my grave under the yew tree,' he said. 'There are some sticks in the ground where I want to be.'

'Father,' the family said as one, 'Father, you are not going to die.'

The doctor's houseboy lit his pipe again and Edward Roberson sat back in his leather-covered chair. 'I've sold my surgical instruments to young Savery. He says that with wooden handles to my knives they can't be sterilized and the instruments are going to a museum.'

Soon after this, my brother and I, on holiday from school, were going to the shop to buy sweets when we heard someone calling for help. The call came from the orchard of Rockland House and we found the doctor lying on the grass beside a five-barred gate. It appeared that he had fallen when he opened the gate. We held the doctor's arms and lifted him on to his feet. He wasn't a big man. He was breathing heavily but we managed to help him into the house. 'Are you Tom Archer's boys?' he asked. 'Yes', we answered. 'I shall write to Tom Archer and tell him how you helped me.' He did write to Dad.

Barbara looked after him and put her father in the hands of Dr Mearns Savery of Evesham, who did what he could for the aged man, but he could see that the end was near. She arranged the funeral at the church. Bunch played the organ and Eward Roberson's death left a gap in the village community which could never be filled. It's true he hadn't been very active during his last years but he was always there at Rockland House, as he had been for so long. There to advise and comfort the old village families, and the children he had brought into the world. Although in many ways a controversial figure, he was almost worshipped by the old folk. Now the ills of the men, women and children of the soil would be dealt with by doctors from Winchcombe, Tewkesbury or Evesham, in smart suits and driving smart cars. No more the cloudy mixture in bottles covered with white paper and sealing-wax. Gone was a man for his time.

Barbara took over the household, cooked for the boys and ran her shop, but all too soon she ailed and slipped away like a cloud passing. She would be missed. Now there were four – Mary, Buckram, Moncrief and Ruth, and soon Ruth would be married.

## RUTH

Ruth, or Cissy, as she was known, was the youngest of the girls. To say she was a rural Madonna would be no exageration, for she was beautiful to the extreme. In a village where plainness was the rule and beauty was the exception, Ruth stood out, a Miss Gloucestershire of the 1920s.

She had many admirers. At a time when cars were rare – one to a village, like parish churches – Ruth, dressed in the height of fashion, took her seat beside the young motorists of Gloucestershire. One smart young man from Stratford-on-Avon thought he would claim her for his bride, but that was not to be. He had a smart furniture store in town and was a pioneer salesman of wireless sets. He drove the twenty miles to court Ruth often, in a Morris Cowley two seater car with dickey seat. I gather that Moncrief, who kept a weather eye on her, didn't like the Stratford gentleman.

Our pasture land under the hill was approached by a cart road at Ayles Acre, or as some said, Hells Acre. The council road beside Ayles Acre rose steeply alongside the Bank Piece. At the summit of Ayles Acre Bank the cart track began, through a gateway where the grass verge is wide enough to park a car off the road. Mr H. from Stratford had arranged to meet Ruth just there, away from Rockland House, away from

Moncrief's eyes. It was a summer evening and the boughs of ripening plums hung low at Ayles Acre. The wood where the rhododendrons were in purple bloom was three fields away. The warmth of the summer evening caused Ruth and her lover to dwell awhile under the plum trees, shaded from the sun, pillowed and mattressed by the grass. The night was young and they would enjoy the scent of the wild thyme on Bredon after sunset.

A rival came along on horseback. He recognized the car and his spirits sank. The horseman, who had often had the pleasure of the company of this beautiful girl, was jealous. He rode his horse up the cart track towards the wood, a road he knew so well for he hunted that hill with the Croome hounds often. From his saddle he noticed something under the plum boughs. Stopping his horse he recognized Ruth's floral headscarf. Her golden shoulder-length hair lay like an untied sheaf of corn against the blue blazer of the Stratford man. 'You deceiver, you deceiver!' he shouted. Ruth and her boyfriend ran towards the wood as the horseman jumped the hedge into the orchard.

The lovers followed the brook, sheltered by withy trees, and plunged into the wood, hiding in a big rhododendron bush. The horseman that day, like many days with the hunt, lost scent of his quarry and in temper rode furiously towards the parked car. He tied his horse to the gatepost and, making quite sure the car belonged to the Stratford businessman, he opened the offside door. The motor stood on the grass verge and in front of the radiator the Ayles Acre Bank dropped steeply towards Carrants Brook at the bottom. Here the road veered sharply to the right. The horseman thought that by releasing the hand brake and pushing the car to the decline in the road it should end its career in the brook. He released the brake, walked to the rear of the car and pushed against the dickey seat. Slowly at first, the car moved down the hill. Then the speed accelerated until by the time it reached the foot of the hill it was travelling at twenty miles an hour. Mounting the grass the Morris Cowley came to rest with its front wheels in the brook and the dickey seat up in the air.

Untying his mount, the horseman rode home to the next village thinking that revenge is sweet. How the businessman got home to Stratford is not known. Moncrief, when he heard of the car incident, pleaded with the doctor to keep a tighter rein on his young daughter. But Dr Roberson was an old man, and Ruth was his ewe lamb.

By the fireside at supper Moncrief continuously referred to the shortness of Ruth's skirts. 'She is a disgrace to the Roberson family,' he called out one evening when Ruth was showing more of the upper part of her leg than was usual with country girls.

Soon the cars ceased to come to the village to take Ruth to the hill or the opera house. She was courted by a steady farmer from the next village, a son of the soil whose ancestors had farmed the land almost as long as the Baldwyns.

I cannot speak too highly of the man she chose to marry, for when my father died he was one whose advice on farming was invaluable. Ruth bore him two sons who carry on the traditions of their father. They work hard, long hours, and farm like their Dad did, rearing claves, growing corn, farrowing a few sows, farming a hundred acres and not poisoning the land with chemicals.

Ruth's only daughter is as pretty as her mother, a lady of great charm, a connoisseur of clothes, of taste, of fashion. She is a woman of character for in her veins flows the blood of the Baldwyns, the Robersons and her dear Dad, the yeoman farmer.

## EDWARD BUCKRAM

The doctor's eldest son was always known as Buckram. During his lifetime he had been a farmer dairyman, and a sportsman who, like his father, was an excellent shot. He was a man whose life was blighted by the death of his mother before he had the chance to establish himself. It's true his father lived until Buckram was twenty-six years old, but the doctor was an old man and with his practice and his other commitments he took little interest in guiding Buckram or his younger brother into business or the art and mystery of farming the land. As a youth Buckram took charge of the farm. He bought a small herd of North Devon heifers and at twenty years of age, when the heifers produced crossbred Hereford calves by our bull, Buckram began his career as a dairyman.

With his churn on a milk float and Bob between the shafts he retailed milk to the villagers. Buckram soon became a feature of village life, carrying the milk bucket with a pint and quart measure slung on its brass looped handle.

The Roberson custom of late rising was passed down to Buckram. He was late all day, every day. He became known as the 'Midnight Milkman'. Buckram had a deep bass singing voice, and I have often heard him singing those old harvest hymns at the midnight hour – 'All is safely gathered in, free from sorrow free from sin' – his midnight music accompanied by the clanking milk pail and the sound of Bob grazing the roadside verge.

The empty jugs were put out on the cottage doorsteps at bedtime. When the men of the land rose at dawn, the pints and quarts of milk were there covered by blue slates as a protection from the night's prowling cats. Only Mr Sandford was still not gone to bed. He would be practising on his cottage organ. Saturdays were the exception, as Buckram milked his cows early and delivered to his customers before tea-time. In smart Norfolk jacket, lovat breeches, polished boots and leggings, Buckram would be bound for Cheltenham in the car he had bought to chauffeur the doctor around. The brass-radiatored motor had 'Britain' as legend under the radiator cap – I have never seen one of that make anywhere. Sacco, his friend, dressed in blazer and flannels with a gaudy bow tie, rode beside Buckram in the two-seater with wooden spoked wheels and shining brass headlamps. Sometimes they went to the Opera House, and other times to the Daffodil Cinema.

When the first house spilled out its patrons, Buckram and Sacco walked to Lower Docham at the bottom end of High Street. Here at a well-known pub they sampled the fleshpots of Down Town, a haunt of pedlars, street traders, dealers, etc., and with the sovereigns in his pocket Buckram bought his pleasures of Saturday night Cheltenham.

More than once I've seen this flaxen haired farmer with a painted lady in the gardens of Rockland House. Here was a young man with a dual personality – the Beau Brummel of Saturdays, walking the Cheltenham Promenade with his current lady, and the harvest-hymn-singing milkman. Unshaven in the week with his everlasting Woodbine and his dung-caked trousers, Buckram was transformed on Saturdays into the straight-backed man in Lovat tweed, with Bryl-creamed hair and a cigar. Some said Buckram had a tile loose, but no, it was he who had the last laugh. His twisted humour was misunderstood. Local knowledge handed down from his ancestors gave him the edge on natives and foreigners alike.

One day Buckram brought two of his cows to our yard. Only one of them was bulling, but two animals drove so much easier than one. Samson, our bull, mounted and served the one cow that our cowman said was on with herself. He served her the second time just to make sure. Buckram said with his wry smile, 'I'll have the other cow served too, it will save me a journey another time.'

Tom looked at me and looked at the cow. He knew Buckram was not serious . . . 'Now get off up that road with your cows and don't thee talk so damn stupid. You know very well the cow's not bulling.' These words were not unexpected, but the young dairyman's suggestion that our bull would show any interest in a cow not in season showed him up as being more of a knave than a fool. Buckram was no fool. He had a bunch of young store cattle for sale at the doctor's. He advertised them in the local journal and after selling them to Hubert, a cattle dealer, he sold them to another farmer. Of course he had to pay the money back to the second purchaser, but little ploys like this gave Buckram a name as not only a midnight milkman but a daytime comedian, always wheeling and dealing, buying and selling in the market or the farms. Buckram bought half a dozen Cheviot ewes from Scotland. In July he drove them down to our yard, for he knew that Shepherd Tidmarsh had been dipping our lambs.

'Dip my ewes will you, Shepherd.'

Alf Tidmarsh leant on his crook by the side of the dipping bath and taking the short clay pipe from between his lips he spat a carefully aimed shot into the yellow ocre coloured sheep-dip. No quarter for Buckram or anyone else from the shepherd – he was gaffer on sheep dipping day. The policeman stood by his side at the compulsory dip. 'Have you given notice to the Bobby here?' Alf said rather caustically. Buckram smiled an innocent smile. He, whose family had farmed the land for 500 years, thought himself above petty form-filling or any kind of officialdom. The policeman produced a form and handed it to Buckram.

'I shan't dip your ewes until they have been sheared, so get them jackets off, understand.' Buckram made the excuse that he had no shears, but Alf lent him a pair.

'There's a drop of good perry at Rockland House. When you are by, you're welcome to a drink,' said Buckram.

'Thank you, but get and shear those sheep before we finish dipping for today.'

The sheep were sheared by him in the cattle shed. Not a tidy job, but they lost their fleeces. Our shepherd laughed at Buckram's attempt at shearing, for the man was no hand at sheep.

'They be as rough as forest ponies,' he said to the policeman, 'but we'll have 'em through the bath.'

Buckram put his six Cheviots in the pen and said there was a question he wanted to ask the shepherd.

'Come on then, let's have it,' was the old man's reply.

'What's the difference between a sheep which has been sheared expertly and well and one like my ewes?'

'A rough job,' the shepherd replied.

'No, just a month,' was Buckram's answer. 'You see,' he said, 'in a month's time, when the wool has grown, who will know the difference between your shearing and mine?'

'Let's have 'em,' was the shepherd's order, and the six ewes had to be immersed, each for one minute, in Cooper's sheep-dip to keep them free from sheep scab and to ward off the blue arsed fly and maggots.

The road from the village street to Buckram's cow ground and his cowshed was long and rough. From where Mr Higgins' blacksmith shop stood years ago, Blacksmiths Lane led to the Little Piece, Under Meadow and beyond. A level crossing over the branch railway line linked Under Meadow and the cow ground. It was not a busy line, yet a hazard for the Midnight Milkman and Bob, his nag. The banana train from Avonmouth rattled along the track every night when the man and his float would cross the line.

Another way to Buckram's field was down Pig Lane, past Land Close Cottage, and over yet another crossing on the railway line. In fact the farm had been split by the coming of the railway in 1864. New Piece, an arable field, was on the village side of the line, while the pastures were on the other. In New Piece Buckram grew marigolds for the cows and some oats. He was no arable farmer, always ploughing late, planting late and harvesting late. I well remember him coming to the yard with Bob and the float to borrow our Ransome horse plough to work his land. I don't know to this day what he did with that plough, for he returned it in pieces, the body apart from the tails and the wheels. Mr Bailey, Dad's partner, was there when he brought it back and I remember the look on his face. 'What the nation have you done to our plough,' he spluttered.

Buckram took a new route to the cow ground. Perhaps he was afraid of getting stuck on the level crossing, I don't know, but he now drove down to the main road and then took a short cut across Pecked Meadow. Pecked Meadow stood un-grazed for months and by winter the foggage of long grass was valuable help over the hungry months, wintering strong store cattle. Dad and his partner, Mr Bailey, rented Pecked Meadow for the season from the landlord.

I helped Tom Whittle, the cowman, to take twenty strong store cattle there one Saturday morning in early January. Buckram's route took him through the road-side gate into Pecked Meadow, and he was constantly leaving this gate open. Several times our heifers escaped into the road. The gate at the low ground end of Pecked Meadow was also often open, and Dick, the black half-legged gelding, strayed into the meadow.

'Buckram,' the landlord said to him, 'Dick has strayed into Pecked Meadow.' Always the comic, Buckram answered, 'That horse does not belong to me it belongs to the doctor.' The doctor had been dead for four years, and the landlord had no idea how to contact him, but such was Buckram's wild way.

The open gate to the main road was dangerous and Shepherd Tidmarsh, who went daily to Pecked Meadow to look after the heifers, decided that there was only one answer to the problem. Provided with lock and chain the shepherd padlocked the gate.

Buckram came and seeing his route was impeded he lifted the gate from its hinges and drove his float through. The shepherd was not to be beaten, and next day he put another padlock and chain round the hinge end of the gate. Buckram arrived and found his way blocked. He went to his cowshed and came back with an axe, beating the lock until it opened. The landlord brought a summons against Buckram for trespass and damages to the lock and the gate.

One thing about the dairyman which sticks in my memory was his ability to walk great distances at a great pace. As Buckram walked towards the court on the morning of the Petty Sessions, he was overtaken by Mr Bailey in his new Hillman car. He was taking the shepherd to court as witness to the petty crime, so he stopped and offered Buckram a lift. 'No thank you. I prefer walking,' came the reply. Buckram pleaded guilty to the charge and paid the ten pounds fine in sovereigns.

Buckram was not daunted by the court case. His smile shone through his blond whiskers. The nightly clank of buckets and the singing was to the old villagers a sign of the continuity of the Baldwyn – Roberson line. Buckram remained heir to Rockland House. He made cider from the orchard trees and perry from the two giant pear trees, one opposite

Rockland House, another in front of the doctor's dispensery.

The hand-reared pheasants from the wood were unlucky if they strayed into the gorse and bramble of the doctor's hill. Buckram's twelve-bore kept a tidy weekend pantry of game. He had hunted with the Croome as a boy when his mother was alive, but now, with the little farm to be worked, he rarely followed the hounds. Yet when the 'view-halloo' sounded by Cuckoo Pen or the Nap, Buckram followed on foot.

Two more milkmen delivered in the village, but despite their tidy brass churns and their shining stainless steel buckets Buckram survived. The old folk remained loyal to the Midnight Milkman. My Uncle George and Aunt Annie had Buckram's milk and I well remember one Sunday night their milk was delivered on the doorstep at one o'clock in the morning.

'Is this morning or evening delivery?' Uncle called from his bedroom window. Buckram's heavy boots clattered down the stone path from Uncle's cottage while Uncle listened in the still air of the early morning. 'We plough the fields and scatter the good seed on the land.' Bob was waiting between the shafts of the float. He had adapted himself to be a night owl like his master. He wouldn't be required until ten o'clock the next morning.

The cowshed housed the four cows (there was room for no more than six). A room at the end of the shed served as a dairy, if one could call it a dairy, and there he kept cattle-cake and various items of harness. Outside, the hayrick stood under the hedge. The cows drank from a pond where the tadpoles turned to frogs every summer, when the croaking of these delightful creatures made music among the new-mown hay as they migrated from pond to pond. The milk was poured directly from his bucket into a churn and was delivered warm from the cows. Unhygienic you may say, yet wasn't the winner at the local baby show fed on Buckram's milk?

Buckram's old-fashioned dairy practice succeeded in shocking some of the new villagers, who were used to clinical milk from bottles, pasteurized, TB free, germ free. His milk was rich and creamy, equal to the Channel Island milk. His Devon cows didn't create records in production but they did give a product which was right in its time. A happy man, yet a loner, Buckram was always striving for something yet unexplored in his life. Why not breed turkeys in the garden of Rockland House? Why not, he thought, and soon he was in business, breeding not only turkeys but guinea-fowl as well. Their plaintive chat, 'Come Back, Come Back' could be heard coming from the garden.

The turkey project was not a success. The land lay wet and heavy, and a disease known as Black Head resulted in the loss of many birds. The guinea-fowl were a success. They roosted at night in the pear tree near the road. The village near Rockland House became yet more alive at midnight, for now Buckram's harvest hymns and clanking milk buckets were accompanied by the 'Come Back, Come Back' of what were known locally as 'gleanys'. How was this man to kill a guinea-fowl for his dinner or for sale in the pub. There was just one way; a shot from his twelve-bore, which would fell a young bird from its perch, creating more noise and confusion amongst the other birds.

Blackberry bushes competed with the grass in the wild garden and orchard of Rockland House. It was a difficult orchard to mow, even with Buckram's one-horse mowing machine. He laboured away one summer with a scythe but the bushes continued to grow so he bought what was to be the answer to his problem. In Beckford market one Tuesday, four young nanny-goats and one bill stood invitingly in the sheep-pens. Goats were cheap in the thirties, sheep were cheap, and lambs were fifteen shillings each. 'Goats,' mused Buckram, 'I wonder how much.' Mr Moore, the auctioneer, had no bids for the goats in the sale ring. 'Not sold,' he said.

The owner was a lady from Coombe Hill who had to get rid of them. Buckram stood by the sheep-pen. 'How much?' he said to the lady. 'Make me an offer,' she replied. Buckram took two golden sovereigns from his pocket. His offer was accepted and soon, when the goats kidded, Buckram was able to offer goats' milk to his customers as an extra. The medical profession had discovered that goats' milk suited children who were allergic to cows' milk.

A young billy kid reared by the dairyman made a succulent dinner for Buckram and his brother and sisters at Rockland House. After skinning the young goat Buckram thought what a waste it was to throw the skin away. In his late father's library were books on all features of the countryside and country living. Here were instructions on the various ways of salting a bacon pig, rearing pheasants, stuffing and mounting wild birds, and curing skins.

Buckram nailed the goat skin flat on a stable door. He scraped off the fat and loose tissue then applied a coating of alum. In a few weeks the inside of the skin went hard and tough, and crackled like parchment when handled. A dressing of glycerine made it pliable, and Buckram cut out a pattern in stiff brown paper – a pattern of a waistcoat.

Soon the Midnight Milkman was seen on his rounds wearing a goat-skin waistcoat over his now tatty Norfolk jacket. He presented a picture of a hairy twentieth- century Esau delivering the rich Devon milk, the sandy goat-skin toning in with his whiskers, singing the harvest hymns between puffs on his eternal Woodbine – quite an unwholesome combination for a milk roundsman, yet his few customers remained faithful to what they termed 'a native among natives'.

Despite Ministry regulations on milk production, an unhygienic Buckram survived with his four cows and his fields adjoining Pecked Meadow. In the 1930s cowsheds had to be correct in every way to satisfy the Ministry. There was, however, a loophole; a loophole exercised by many smallholders in Somerset. It was still legitimate to milk cows standing in the field; Buckram took advantage of this old practice. His cows were quiet, and knew their names; Buckram was like a brother to them. He milked his cows in the field, carrying his stool and bucket to where they stood. His pasture was so much cleaner than his cowshed. Tuberculin testing was in its infancy, yet many herds were becoming attested. Buckram had no time for vets and no hyperdermic syringe ever planted serums or vaccines into his cows. He had a distant cousin, the well known character Laughing Tom, who would come and assist when a cow calved.

Along the beam of the cowshed the old remedies used by generations of Baldwyns were still in bottle and packet. Cataline, Pettefers Mixture, linseed oil, turpentine, Stockholm tar. In the cow ground great lumps of rock salt shone in the sunshine, pink, brown, and white where the cows had licked the minerals, minerals so important for health.

As the war clouds grew blacker over Europe and the government realised how dependent we were as an island community on imported foods, change was on its way. Once more, farmers were to become the blue-eyed boys in an industrialized, chiefly town-dwelling country. The country would need more home-grown food. The Minister of Agriculture, Mr W.S. Morrison, introduced subsidies on lime and basic slag. A wise move on his part, as the farmers could get lime and slag at a very cheap rate. This applied to pasture land improved it greatly, and when the great ploughing-up campaign came into force the improved grass sward had inbuilt fertility resulting in good crops of grain on ploughed pasture.

Buckram was cynical when his neighbours dressed their fields with cheap, simple minerals. He would depend as always on the muck from his cowshed. Four more young heifers had wintered in there providing the manure for his potato patch and for growing his marigolds. 'Slag on my fields,' he said, 'what, the left-overs from the steel works at Bilston? Never. Slag kills mushrooms, and my mushrooms are a cash crop.' He remembered what had happened at Sabberton thirty years ago when slag put paid to all the mushrooms on the farms.

Although Buckram was the doctor's eldest son, he had much of his mother's Baldwyn blood in his veins. The Baldwyns had farmed a great part of the parish for more years than could be counted. Some said it was five hundred years, while the local oracle, known as Henry Fly By Night, said it was before the rememberance of man. They farmed in an unhurried fashion. No one could ever alter their pattern. Pigs were fed until they oozed of fat; plums and pears were never picked until they were completely ripe or mellow – 'mella', the locals said. Buckram, who never read a newspaper or listened to the radio, probably heard in the Teddington Hands, a pub that he preferred, that we were at war on 3 September 1939. No war, no government was ever going to alter his life-style. Twice a day milking, picking his fruit, gathering mushrooms and blackberries for market, making cider. Hadn't all his Baldwyn ancestors done just that? His fifteen acres of pasture near Pecked Meadow and his seven acres of arable in New Piece were his empire. The harvest of 1939 saw Buckram picking his fruit as usual then delivering the midnight milk.

Soon after the outbreak of war, the War Agricultural Committee was formed in every county. The County

Committee then formed District Committees. The members of the District Committee were mostly farmers or retired farmers, and my experience of them was that they were on the whole men of ability who worked under a District Officer, usually an agricultural college graduate. The committee had powers to dictate to farmers what crops were to be grown on their land. Farmers were graded into Grade A, B and C. Grade A was the top grade of farm; Grade B, medium farms, not just a medium farmer but his land not capable at that time to produce good crops; Grade C were farms under supervision, farms usually run by either inexperienced men or older dog-and-stick farmers.

Much has been said and written about War Agricultural Committees. Wentworth Day in his book, *Harvest Adventure*, writes about the Fascist-like activities of the Essex Committee. In Worcestershire I found the officers reasonable, tempered always by the committee members who had a very close contact with the land. There were exceptions and my father, who was a member of a District Committee, did succeed in preventing the Executive Committee dispossessing an old farmer of the Vale.

Mr X farmed two hundred and fifty acres. He was ordered, as we all were, to grow potatoes on his clay land. Potatoes were needed. Fair enough. By Christmas Mr X's potatoes were still in the ground. The Executive ordered him to lift them in the next three weeks or he would be dispossessed of his land. For three weeks it snowed and froze continually. The potatoes were still in the land. It was impossible to lift poatatoes in those conditions. The Executive pronounced after those three weeks that the farmer should be dispossessed. Dad asked the officer if he could have lifted potatoes in the frost and snow, and succeeded in getting a reprieve for Mr X. Officialdom from an office desk can be insensitive to the work in the field.

Stories abound of the War Ag. There were cases of landlords serving on committees who had sons they wanted to place on farms they owned, and tried to conjure up reasons for the dispossession of one of their tenants. Isolated cases.

Buckram, a free spirit, had never been dictated to since his schooldays under Mr Summerville. He remembered the 1914 war when his doctor father who served on the Medical Board had the power to say whether men went into the army or stayed on the land. He carried on as usual despite the war. Milk, eggs, bacon, vegetables, fruit all at hand, and his special vintage of the Wine of the West – cider.

After milking his four cows, Buckram was engaged in mucking out his cowshed and spreading the muck on his home ground. Two men with papers in their hands and an ordnance survey map walked across the field towards him.

'Good morning. Mr Roberson, I gather. I'm the District Officer of the War Agricultural Committee,' the younger man addressed Buckram.

Buckram eyed the men with suspicion, then said, 'You are trespassing on my land. I was fined ten pounds a while back for coming across Pecked Meadow to my fields. What have you got to say?'

The District Officer then informed Buckram that they had powers under the government to inspect all agricultural land. The officer and the committee member then told him that he was to plough up the fifteen acres of pasture and plant it with winter wheat.

'They are small fields,' the officer said. 'We can send a bulldozer from our depot at Hinton and push up your hedges and do the ploughing for you.' Buckram was incensed by this encroachment on his life-style, but just told the men that he and his ancestors had farmed the land for five hundred years and what about his four cows?

Some days after the visit the order arrived by post at Rockland House for Buckram to plough his pasture land and plant it with wheat. Moncrief, Buckram's younger brother, had had a good education, partly by a tutor from Cheltenham College and also by study. He was very well up in legal matters. Obviously he was upset when his brother told him of the ploughing-up order. Moncrief said that a lot of the ridge-and-furrow pastures under the hill had been formed by the ploughing-up campaign during the Napoleonic Wars. He knew, and Buckram knew, that their land had never been ploughed. 'It's brookside meadows,' Moncrief said. 'These lush pastures alongside Carrants Brook should never feel the ploughshare. They will be ruined and the winter flooding will destroy any crops. You can appeal, you know, Buckram.'

Buckram declared that there was no need to appeal for he would resist any encroachment on his land. The gate was locked. The fences were reinforced with barbed wire. Buckram's little farm resembled the prisoner of war camp at Sudeley.

Soon the War Ag. sent another order that the land was to be ploughed in time for the autumn planting of wheat. 'I thought we were fighting Hitler. This is dictatorship,' Buckram said to his brother.

The inevitable dispossession order followed from the County Executive Committee. Buckram became more and more worried and vigilant over his farm. He spent his time watching over his acres. Moncrief was supportive to him, but he begged him to leave his twelve-bore gun at Rockland House for he knew that if tempers were raised by visits from the War Agricultural Committee Officers, Buckram may use his gun.

Soon after the dispossession order it became the thankless job of the District Officer to arrange for one of his tractors to plough up Buckram's land. The committee had an agricultural machinery depot at Hinton about two and a half miles from Buckram's little farms. A young driver was sent with a Standard Fordson tractor and a two-furrow Ransome plough to plough the land, but when he arrived at the farm gate he found it to be locked. The obvious thing to do was to unhang the gate and open it. Looking around the first field with some trepidation the young man walked across to the opposite hedge putting a stick in the ground on the headland. He set his plough and soon the share and mouldboard were turning over the green sward and patterning a brown line straight across the field. He turned on the headland, then ploughed two furrows up against his first furrows, forming a shallow ridge.

Buckram's four cows were inquisitive, they came and viewed the scene. The ploughman set his plough deeper, cutting a furrow slice six inches deep, burying the turf.

Buckram had been to Rockland House and as he leisurely drove down the Groaten with Dick his nag in the milk float he heard the sound of a tractor in his fields. Persuading old Dick into a trot he hurriedly approached his field through the unhinged open gate. 'What are you doing on my land?' he shouted over the noise of the Fordson. The tractor driver stopped his engine. 'I'm ploughing your field by order of the War Ag.,' he replied.

Buckram fetched a hedge hook from the bed of his milk float and said, 'Get off my land or I'll use this on you.' The tractor driver jumped from his machine and ran into the road while Buckram stood with his weapon in hand, guarding his property.

From the kiosk in the village the young tractor driver phoned his depot and the District Officer phoned the local policeman. The police obtained a warrant for Buckram's arrest while a magistrate and doctor signed an order to commit the Midnight Milkman to the County Mental Hospital as a compulsory patient. Two special constables and the policeman arrived at Rockland House to arrest Buckram. Buckram left the house by the back door, running up the orchard to what he thought was the safety of Bredon Hill.

It happened that the village boys from school were on holiday and seeing the police running after Buckram they joined in the chase. Buckram ran at a cracking pace to the Cuckoo Pen on Little Hill. He was an outdoor man, fit and hardy. From the Cuckoo Pen, Buckram ran to the corner of Grafton Firs. He lay here among the elderflower like a fox gone to ground. The pack of police and boys closed on the Firs. Buckram, with that saucy grin on his face, broke cover running towards Great Hill Barn. He rested awhile there.

Buckram knew the hill so well, every tree was familiar to him. From the barn the pack chased their prey down Furze Hill through the wood and the American Orchard, into the doctor's hill. As he ran down the village street two more special constables closed on him at the chapel. Fastening his grip on the iron gate of the chapel Buckram refused to move. Despite persuasion from the police, Buckram held on to that gate for hours. The police car waited to take him to the mental hospital, but Buckram was adamant he was going to stay.

Among the bevy of folk outside the chapel was Bill Vale, an old friend and contempory of Buckram's. He volunteered to accompany the Midnight Milkman in the car to the hospital. Obviously Buckram was in a state of shock, grasping at straws, most of all his freedom was at stake. At last he loosed his grip of the gate saying, 'Well, if Bill's going, I'll come with him.' Sadly Buckram left the village, never to return.

# BILL'S STORY

I often wonder how Bill Vale persuaded Buckram to
get into the police car. Bill was never reckoned to be
one of the cleverest of chaps. Apart from being a keen
supporter of the local football team, he was a quiet,
ordinary farm worker. The police failed to get the
midnight milkman into the car, the special constables
present, all near neighbours of Buckram, were help-
less. Buckram stood adamant with his hands clutching
the upright iron bars of the chapel gate. I wonder
whether he thought that being on the grounds of a
religious house he was safe. His ancestors no doubt
had found sanctuary in the churches and abbeys of the
Vale when under threat from the law.

When Bill Vale whispered something in Buckram's
ear he loosed the gate and took his seat in the back of
the car beside his old friend. 'What did you tell him?'
the local policeman asked Bill.

'That's my business,' came the curt answer. And so
it was Bill's business. Why should he disclose to the
so-called professionals the commonsense suggestion he
made to Buckram.

When the car arrived at the mental hospital Buckram was interviewed in reception with Bill in attend-
ance. The psychiatrist who talked with him turned to
Bill and said, 'I understand there was difficulty in
persuading my patient to come to the hospital. How
did you manage it my friend?'

Bill explained that Buckram had lost his farm to the
War Agricultural Committee and was very upset in
consequence. He told the medical man exactly what he
said to Buckram, which was, 'Come with me, Buckram, to Worcester and we'll see if we can't get your
farm back off the War Ag.' It worked. As the Book

says, 'out of the mouths of babes and sucklings', Bill
had a word in season. Buckram when he arrived at the
mental hospital was in his working clothes, unshaven,
unwashed. The nurses were kind but firm with their
new patient. After a hot bath he agreed to be shaved by
one of the male nurses. The following day he had a
haircut.

Life for him had changed. The outdoor life on his
farm had been food and drink for him. A brother to his
cows, a man who often slept the night away on his
hay-rick under the stars. One concludes that the
restriction of four walls was as a prison to Buckram.
He had lived a healthy life in his way. Feeding on the
bacon, the eggs, drinking the rich milk from his Devon
cows, walking miles, for he was a great walker; Buckram thought nothing of walking the six miles to
Evesham or eight miles to Tewkesbury. I would see
him striding along, a yard at a time to town. Now this
caged bird whimpered like a puppy in an antiseptic
centrally heated ward. Once a free spirit, now a broken
spirit. Moncrief visited him. He came away knowing
that Buckram would never bend to rules, never settle
in hospital. 'That's not my brother,' Moncrief said to
one of the nurses.

He described his brother Buckram to me. He was
squat in the corner of the little ward, refusing to speak
to anyone. The nurses had difficulty in persuading him
to eat anything. He had shrunk into a bent old man,
his will to live had left him.

The inevitable happened. Buckram developed
pneumonia. Why, you may ask, for wasn't he a hardy
outdoor creature, outdoor in all winds and weathers?
Here the ward was hygienically clean, centrally heated,
the food was reasonable, as reasonable as wartime
rations would allow. The nurses were caring. One
thing he lacked. His freedom. Nothing would compen-
sate for that. No doubt the pneumonia was caused by

Buckram

Moncrief, 1928

shock and Buckram's resistance was at a low ebb. In the days before antibiotics his condition worsened. It's doubtful whether antibiotics would have saved him. Buckram died sixteen miles away from the Bredon Hill he loved.

He is buried in the churchyard by the moat pond at Ashton-under-Hill, where a stone marks the spot. It states his age; forty. He died because he refused to conform with government orders. No blame on the hospital – they had the problem of trying to restore an outdoor man in a ward. Were the War Agricultural Committee to blame? They had to be ruthless in wartime, yet it was like using a cannon to kill a fly.

# WILLIAM HENRY MONCRIEF

W.H.M. Roberson, known as Creef, attended the village school at Ashton-under-Hill. The headmaster at that time, 1913–1916, was A.S. Somerville. After having private tuition from Aylmer Strong of Cheltenham, Creef applied for various posts, and Somerville was first to give him a good reference. In answer to a questionaire from the Colonial Office, Aylmer Strong wrote as follows:

The Private Secretary (Appointments)
Colonial Office.
34 Promenade, Cheltenham          21st Dec., 1926

Dear Sir,
Understanding that a brief statement of the nature of his occupation since February of this year would be of service to W.H.M Roberson for submission to your department.

I wish to say that during five months of the period in question Mr Roberson was reading substantially with me for the Civil Service Examination jointly with the Army Exam. He worked with all the keenness and application which he has displayed during the three years he has been with me.

During the remainder of the period he was residing in his father's house, reading, haymaking, shooting and generally keeping himself physically fit. He has now resumed his regular reading with me.

Yours faithfully,
Aylmer Strong

Strong wrote to Creef's father as follows:

Dear Dr Roberson,
I was sorry to hear from Creef today that the prospects for the exam for the Civil Service are so unsatisfactory. That exam ought to have been well within his competence.

It is hard to know what to advise in these days. Everything at home is so overcrowded. All the professions seem to be stiffening their qualifications. India is becoming less and less of a white man's dwelling place.

If you have any influence with anyone who could help in putting him into a promising business post in this country, I'd go for that. He talked with some enthusiasm today about the possibilities in Australia under the state aided scheme. I'm not sure something like that might be best of all.

Your boy is a real good fellow whom it is a pleasure to help in his work. He has come on very well indeed with his French and has put great energy and application into his task. I consider he has shown real grit and determination. I'm glad to tell you so.

Yours sincerely,
Aylmer Strong

Despite really good testimonials from Revd Fowler, Vicar of Elmley Castle, and from his brother-in-law, Fred Kempton, Creef never got into the Civil Service, local government or the law. A great mind lost to what could have been ideal for him.

Creef settled down at last to the role of a small farmer. He was never intended to be like Buckram, who was a simple rural swain tied to the cow's tail. Creef was very knowledgeable of the law and languages. He spoke and wrote fluent French, but he turned his attention to turkey farming. He kept the American Mammoth Bronze birds in his orchard. All went well for him until a particularly wet summer affected his small flock with Black Leg, a disease which, in those pre-antibiotic days, killed off the young stock.

He bought an old post office van to take his produce to market. In his orchard there were some choice varieties of apples, plums and pears. Picking the tall trees was no problem to him. Often have I seen Creef on the top rungs of a forty rung ladder swaying in the autumn gales picking his pears.

The blackberries on the hill were the province of the wives of the farm men. They made a little money harvesting these 'fruits for free'. My cousin Tom bought them and packed them in baskets, sending the fruit to the markets of the north. Creef never thought it odd for a doctor's son to join forces with the village women in gathering the blackberry harvest.

His free-range eggs found a good market and so did his Christmas turkeys and cockerels. Creef kept up a tradition of the Baldwyn family in rearing the broad-breasted game cockerels for the table. He planted Christmas trees in his paddock and always placed a tall tree near the front door of Rockland House, illuminated by coloured lights during the Christmas season.

When the Second World War came Creef worked on the fruit farms of Teddington and Alderton. This was his war effort. The local policeman, the same officer who had chased Buckram over the hill, visited Creef at Rockland House. 'You are to report to the Home Guard and do your duty on the hill.'

Creef looked the man in the face and said, 'But for that uniform, I'd thrash you out into the road.' Creef told him, 'Go on your way. I'm not joining the Home Guard and you should know why.'

This brother of Buckram did not forget the War Ag. dispossession order which had robbed the family of their farm. He had registered as a conscientious objector, and was therefore not liable for military service.

As the policeman walked away down the road, Creef shouted after him, 'Take that tunic off and I'll fight you for a fiver!'

The Home Guard had a hut near the Cuckoo Pen on Bredon Hill, where they performed guard duty at dawn and dusk. The hill was Creef's second love, and during the early years of the war, on mild summer nights he would sleep on the turf, rolled up in his sleeping-bag. Some members of the Home Guard reported him, saying that he may have been signalling to the enemy planes. This was ridiculous, but the report had to go to H.Q. The officer who went to see Creef accepted his explanation for sleeping on the hill.

The village spies kept watch on Creef. He had a powerful radio set and as he was fluent in German, Italian and Russian, he would spend winter nights listening to broadcasts from the Continent. 'He's a Fifth Columnist,' a few of the spies said, but Creef was as loyal to the Crown as his mother had been in the First World War. The two Italian prisoners who lived on my farm were very taken with Creef. Here was a man who could speak their language. Guiseppe and Pedro helped Creef to pick his pears on Saturday afternoons, and he enjoyed their friendship, for he had few friends in the village.

When the Second World War ended Creef was in the forefront of volunteers who worked in the refugee camps in Europe. He laboured unstintingly among the sick and starving in the bomb-blasted towns and cities on the Continent. On his return, the inevitable flow of letters came to Rockland House from the people he had helped. The foreign stamped mail again was viewed with suspicion, and again the accusation of being a spy came from someone who should have known better. Creef was dedicated to a world of peace, and was instrumental in forming a branch of the International Friendship League.

By the late 1950s my eleven acres of young plum trees were coming into bear. Among the folk who helped to pick the fruit in my orchard by the wood on the hill was Creef. As I have said, he was a good chap with a ladder. He brought his sister Mary with him and she picked the lower branches off the ground. They never started work before teatime. That was the time of day peculiar to the Robersons.

In the field next to the plum orchard I had planted wheat. It had been a pasture filed known as Holbrook. This was the first year it had been cropped, and after the corn had been combined and the straw baled, I took my laying hens to feed on the stubble, housing them at night in fold units. Every evening I went and shut them up safe from marauding foxes. One evening it was late when I went to close the doors on the fowl pens. The moon was already shining full over the Cotswolds. After shutting up my hens I thought I saw something moving at the top of the plum trees. Walking nearer, Creef called 'Good night Fred, what a lovely moon.' I said, 'You can't see to pick plums this time of night can you?' Mary from beneath the tree said, 'Oh, yes Freddy, we can see.'

This man, Moncrief, who should have gained a post as head of a department in the Civil Service, picked my plums under the moon. I think of him as Matthew Arnold's Scholar Gypsy, a man who joined the Romanies, his studies never completed. Yet Creef, who had a great affection for gypsies, chose to be a loner. Often the gypsy caravans stayed overnight in his fields as they helped with the hay making. Matthew Arnold writes in 'The Scholar Gypsy':

Still nursing the unconquerable hope,
Still clutching the inviolable shade,
With a free, onward impulse brushing through,
By night, the silvered branches of the glade
Far on the forest-skirts where none pursue.
On some mild pastoral slope
Emerge, and resting on the moonlit pales
Freshen thy flowers as in former years
With dew, or listen with enchanted ears
From the dark dingles, to the nightingales.

A true description of Moncrief, a solitary, who drank deeply the delights of Bredon Hill. Sunshine and shade aptly describes his life.

The shade became a darkness in 1964, for Moncrief endured yet another disappointment. He was more of a son of his mother, a Baldwyn, than a Roberson. Moncrief was proud of the Baldwyn line. He would recite the family tree to me. They had built the little hamlet of Paris, and maybe the shepherd's house on the summit of Bredon known as La Lu, was built by them.

Moncrief used to talk of one bell in the belfry which he called the Baldwyn bell. When the bells had been re-hung in 1964, Moncrief joined the team of learner ringers. What happened in the belfry at one practice is not clear, except that Moncrief did insist on ringing the Baldwyn bell. The next day he received a letter from the Church Warden telling him he was not to go to the belfry and that he was ringing dangerously. He came to see me after he had destroyed the letter. He was distraught, but I did say it was a pity he destroyed the letter because to me it sounded libellous. I tried to impress upon him not to go to the belfry. He said, 'But all bells are Baldwyn bells, they paid Rudalls of Gloucester for them.'

The incident was reported in the *Evesham Journal* of 2 April, 1965:

Man's action after being told no room for you in the belfry.

William Roberson of Rockland House, Ashton-under-Hill, was bound over to keep the peace in the sum of five pounds at Evesham's Magistrates Court on Wednesday. The trouble started after he attempted to join the bell-ringing team at Ashton church, the court was told. He was summoned by Mrs Eunice Stephens, a member of the team and church organist, who told the court that she threatened to resign if Mr Roberson became a member of the team.

Mr Solway, prosecuting for Mrs Stephens, said his client and her daughter, a schoolgirl, were both bell-ringers. On March 10th, they were just leaving their house on their way to the practice when the defendant arrived. He asked her a question and because she detected an argumentative ring in his voice, she stepped back inside her gate. There was then a 'battle of torches' in which they both shone flashlights at each other. The defendant threatened to strike Mrs Stephens and when she stepped out of the way he threatened her daughter. Mrs Stephens' instincts as a mother overcame her fear and she stepped in between them. He said, 'Over garden hedge.'

The next thing she knew was that she received a blow or a push which knocked her sideways over the garden hedge. She finished up on her back with her legs in the hedge. Mrs Stephens of Old Beams, Ashton, said that Mr Roberson said to her, 'I have as much right to go bell-ringing as you. Why can't I go bell-ringing?'

Cross-examined by Mr J.L. Poole, defending, Mrs Stephens said that she felt no animosity towards Mr Roberson, but agreed that she had sent solicitors' letters to him and wanted him to stop speaking to her daughter. She admitted that she objected to him being present during a bell-ringing practise. 'I said if Mr Roberson was to become a member of the bell-ringing team, my daughter and I would quietly withdraw,' she told the court.

As a result a letter was sent from the vicar and church wardens telling Mr Roberson that the belfry was not very large and there was not room for people who were not actually ringing.

Mr Poole: Over the years Mr Roberson's family have had a very close connection with the church?

Mrs Stephens: Yes

Mr Poole: To be told in this manner to keep away from his village church was a matter which was likely to cause him some considerable concern.

Mr Roberson told the court that he had received an invitation to join the bell-ringing team but after attending on a few occasions he received a letter telling him his presence was not welcome. After making inqiries about it he satisfied himself that this was due to Mrs Stephens and he went to see her to make a compromise. She was hysterical. He did not strike her but knocked her torch to one side because it was shining in his face. She tripped and fell backwards over the hedge. The chairman, Mr Henry Ashwin, told him, 'It's all rather a storm in a tea cup. You must not molest people in their gardens, or push ladies through hedges.'

Moncrief was bound over at the Magistrates Court. He related to me the day at the Sessions and said he went early on his Lambretta scooter and called at Hampton church. He remembered the story of how his father, Doctor Roberson, had married Amy Baldwyn by Licence in that church. 'Father could not have travelled secretly along the branch railway line today,' he told me. 'There's no railway line now. Beeching has closed it,' he said. I listened to a man who took comfort from his memory of the past when Baldwyns were everything in the village.

'Why did you go into the church, Creef,' I asked.

'Oh, just to pray to God to guide me,' he said.

Creef had bought land in the village to replace the farm which Buckram had been dispossessed of. He owned Ashton Meadow, Long Dewrest, Middle Dewrest and Little Dewrest. The three Dewrests were pasture where he mowed for hay. Dependent on contractors to bale the hay, it was often spoilt by rain. He planted wheat in Ashton Meadow. Having no time for chemical sprays, he scythed off the thistles. I saw this wirey, tough man swinging a scythe there at sunset cropping off the thistles above the ears of corn in July, enjoying the summer evening.

The kind of farming he was forced into by the doctor was Victorian in style. He cut chaff for the horses by hand. He pulped mangolds with a hand operated root pulper. The lateness of the family ruled their day and night. I remember him as a fearless man on a ladder. He'd be picking pears on the high trees in Rockland orchard in a gale. The ladder would sway like a ship at sea. Creef picked the high branches into his basket. He'd be singing loudly, often an aria from Handel's *Messiah*. He loved his fruit and fruit picking. One consolation, in a way, for farming he didn't enjoy.

He did enjoy cider-making. An old cider mill stood in the fruit garden of Rockland House, a stone mill operated by a horse. Lavender, the Robersons' favourite cob, pushed the stone around the trough by an ancient mechanism. Creef made splendid cider. Doctor Roberson had recommended cider to his patients. His theory was that amid the dust of threshing, lime sowing, slag sowing on the land, cider was good to clear the throat. Creef sold cider in four and a half gallon barrels. He bought genuine cider fruit from neighbours' orchards when he was short of apples.

At various times of the year I picture Creef Roberson. In September on Bredon Hill picking blackberries; he'd be dressed in some of his old clothes amongst the briars, unshaven hatless and singing – a happy man. In October out with Sailor, his dog, shooting rabbits and pigeons in New Piece. Here he grew five acres of sprouts, always late. He picked in March when most farmers had finished. In late November he'd be fetching a load of mangolds from our mangold bury with Lavender and the float. He stored a few of the sugary roots in his barn for the two horses for their bait in spring.

When I last saw my friend Creef he had just discharged himself from hospital. 'I wasn't staying there,' he said. 'Do you know Fred, the nurses gave me two pills to swallow at night. Two pills,' he repeated.

'No doubt they did,' I said.

'I wasn't going to take two pills.' Then he added, 'And the doctors, they were about the ward without a collar or tie, in their shirt sleeves.' He laughed. 'I have no faith in men like that. You remember Father wore a black frock coat, stiff collar, pin-striped trousers and spats?'

'Times have changed, Creef,' I said.

It was obvious that Creef would not accept hospital treatment for what seemed to be an ulcer. At home he became worse and took to his bed. Peritonitis developed and Creef died in his room at Rockland House, where he chose to die. A man who never quite succeeded, yet basically a happy man, a kind man, the last of the gentry of Ashton-under-Hill.

# Muddy Boots and Sunday Suits

Fred Archer

'One of Britain's best loved tellers of stories about the countryside . . . a vivid portrayal of village life and its colourful characters.' *The Citizen*

'Enchanting . . . will delight all those who love the countryside.' *Western Morning News*

'His reminiscences of country life really do have a humour, poetry and curious literary perception of their own.' *Auberon Waugh*

Fred Archer's childhood was spent in the innocent age between the two world wars. Here he brings to life that lost world of summers spent sledging on the grass on the staves of cider barrels, severe Sunday School teachers, and idle hours playing with hoops, pop-guns and catapults. He recalls this time of great change in the village: the coming of the wireless (treated with great suspicion), the last governess cart, replaced by a gleaming tourer; and the arrival of the scrap-iron Jacks, rightly predicting the onset of war and the end of an age in Ashton. An accomplished narrator, his vivid evocation of village life is complemented by photographs from his own collection.

ISBN 0-7509-0961-7 (paperback)

# A Lad of Evesham Vale

*Tales from Country Life*

Fred Archer

'Rich: with humour, kindness, vivacity. And it has a sense of the place, magically conveyed.'       *Guardian*

'His writing goes a long way to restoring some of the right kind of robustness to the recent past.'
*The Countryman*

'the native raconteur par excellence, connecting the generations with racy loops of storytelling, and bringing to robust life a rural world which post-Second World War changes might seem to have buried for ever.'       *Ronald Blythe*

'His reminiscences of country life really do have a humour, poetry and a curious literary perception of their own.'       *Auberon Waugh*

An enchanting menagerie of Worcestershire country folk are gathered together here, from the alluring barmaid Amy Lights – 'a rural Venus' – to the Reverend Vernon, who rides a tricycle 'religiously' and excels at funerals. Central to the tales is Sacco, a builder's apprentice, a scoundrel who seduces the girls and startles the older folk on his much prized motorbike, but a likeable one; he is indeed a true 'lad' of the Vale.

ISBN 0-7509-0962-5 (paperback)